EATING DISORDERS

EATING DISORDERS
Time for Change

Mona Villapiano, Psy.D.
Laura J. Goodman, M.Ed., LMHC

BRUNNER-ROUTLEDGE
ALERE FLAMMAM
Taylor & Francis Group

USA	Publishing Office:	BRUNNER-ROUTLEDGE *A member of the Taylor & Francis Group* 325 Chestnut Street Philadelphia, PA 19106 Tel: (215) 625-8900 Fax: (215) 625-2940
	Distribution Center:	BRUNNER-ROUTLEDGE *A member of the Taylor & Francis Group* 7625 Empire Drive Florence, KY 41042 Tel: 1-800-634-7064 Fax: 1-800-248-4724
UK		BRUNNER-ROUTLEDGE *A member of the Taylor & Francis Group* 27 Church Road Hove E. Sussex, BN3 2FA Tel.: +44 (0) 1273 207411 Fax: +44 (0) 1273 205612

EATING DISORDERS: Time for Change

2 3 4 5 6 7 8 9 0

Printed by George H. Buchanan Co., Philadelphia, PA, 2001.
Cover design by Claire O'Neill
A CIP catalog record for this book is available from the British Library.
∞ The paper in this publication meets the requirements of the ANSI Standard Z39.48-1984 (Permanence of Paper).

Library of Congress Cataloging-in-Publication Data
Villapiano, Mona.
    Eating disorders : time for change / Mona Villapiano, Laura J. Goodman.
        p. ; cm.
    Includes bibliographical references and index.
    ISBN 1-58391-057-3 (paper : alk. paper)
        1. Eating disorders. 2. Eating disorders—Treatment. I. Goodman, Laura J. II. Title.
    [DNLM: 1. Eating Disorders—therapy. 2. Eating Disorders—psychology. 3. Patient Care Planning. 4. Psychotherpay—methods.   WM 175 V718e 2001]
RC552.E18 V54 2001
616.85′26—dc 21

00-049391

ISBN 1-58391-057-3 (paper)

DEDICATION

To my husband, Dr. Albert Villapiano, whose steady love, clinical acumen, and technical skill have enriched my work and my life; and to my most precious daughters, Allison and Alexandra, who help me remember what is important in life.
—Mona Villapiano

To Tobin and Taylor, with love always.
To Elaine: my mother, teacher, and friend.
—Laura J. Goodman

Contents

Acknowledgments

We owe our deepest gratitude to our colleagues Dr. Suetta Tenney and Dr. Julie Balaban for the preparation of Chapter 12, Medical Care, and Chapter 13, Psychopharmacological Issues and Management. Their medical and psychiatric expertise and acumen, respectively, lends credence to chapters that non-medical clinicians alone could not convey.

To our many clients who have taught us over the years to be patient, reflective, and respectful of each unique journey to recovery, we owe our thanks and admiration.

Finally, we thank our families and friends for their love, support, and encouragement.

Preface

Over the years we have read many books about the treatment of eating disorders, attended many lectures, and worked with many clients. Much of what is out there is tremendously helpful. However, many colleagues who attend our lectures are asking for practical information: the "how-to's," worksheets, forms, and helpful hints that only those with years of experience treating clients with eating disorders possess.

With the advent of managed care and the press of time and limited resources, we have heard an outcry from our colleagues who want concrete assistance in developing more efficient and effective treatment plans, interventions, and practices. They are hearing that it is "time for change," but the tools of change have been missing or elusive.

In this dual workbook collection for therapist and client, we present practical, clear, and concrete information, forms, and worksheets to therapists while introducing them to the Stages of Change theory (Prochaska, Norcross, & DiClemente, 1994). For clients, we present a wealth of information and worksheets that they can use alone, in therapy, or as between-session tasks.

The information in this book, *Eating Disorders: Time for Change* is meant to streamline the mental health, medical, and nutritional health professional's work, maximize his or her efficient use of time and resources, and increase his or her efficacy with these clients.

The book offers a simple but comprehensive chart of the stages of change as promulgated by Prochaska and his colleagues (1994) with the addition of the specific tasks and therapeutic approaches professionals might use to help clients with eating disorders achieve their unique goals at each stage of change.

In Chapters 1 through 3, we ask professionals to look at their treatment environments, presentation style, and personal histories to explore how these could advance or detract from their effectiveness in working with these clients. We offer concrete assessment tools and techniques which maximize the gathering of information while minimizing the face-to-face time to gather such data. Our approach encourages full participation from clients and ownership of the process of change. It engenders hope in those who see themselves as failures and sparks the desire to change in those who do not see their eating disorders as problematic.

Special chapters on hunger, food restriction, and binge eating and purging (Chapters 4 through 6) review physiological, psychological, social, and cultural issues related to food and eating while presenting practical forms and worksheets to explore while encouraging self-exploration and practical approaches to effect change.

Chapter 7, Body Image and Weight offers the professional and client an opportunity to address the split between body and self directly through experimental exercises that our clients have found most helpful. It encourages clients to give their bodies a "voice" while subduing the voice of the eating disorder.

Chapter 8, The Athlete, addresses the special and unique circumstances encountered by professionals who work with athletes whose very identity and love of sport is threatened by the eating disorder. It offers forms and worksheets that the client, professional treatment team, and coach can use to formulate goals and measure progress.

The chapters on Substance Abuse and Eating Disorders and Sexual Abuse (Chapters 9 and 10) offer a plan for working with clients with this dyad or triad of diagnoses at one time rather than expecting that clients will hold one symptom complex in abeyance until the other is cured. Practical guidelines, treatment forms, and worksheets help with focus, decrease the overwhelming nature of this work, highlight safety as the primary goal, and offer professionals and clients opportunities to see small gains often overlooked by all-or-nothing approaches to treatment.

The final chapters, Nutritional Counseling, Medical Care, and Psychopharmacological Issues and Management (Chapters 11 through 13) offer comprehensive overviews of nutrition, medical, and medication issues which must be explored, addressed, and monitored for clients with eating disorders. Futhermore, guidelines and helpful approaches to working with clients at all stages of change are offered to enhance the effectiveness of professionals who work with these clients. These chapters, written in layman's terms, help professionals of all disciplines better understand the roles and goals of the other professionals with whom they may be working.

We hope our experience with this approach to the treatment of clients with eating disorders will engender hope and offer practical assistance to you and your clients as you begin the journey to recovery.

Introduction

In eating disorders treatment, frustration often reigns among clinicians. We see immense suffering and are unable to ameliorate it. We see clients not making progress in outpatient treatment sessions and, although progress may be made in inpatient and partial hospital settings, often it is lost upon discharge. We witness the revolving door of clients going in and out of treatment facilities without recovery. We see clients in what appears to be interminable outpatient care only to observe the chronic course of illness setting in. At other times we see clients, against all odds, turning their lives around. We see long courses of suffering melting, finally, into the sweetness of recovery. We see clients on their third, fourth, and fifth hospitalizations, finally breaking free of the bonds of illness. Or we see the client who has given up hope suddenly finding meaning in her life and freeing herself from starvation, bingeing, and purging. When we are truly fortunate, we see our clients valuing their lives, finding their voices, and breaking free of self-destructive behaviors and ways of thinking even when others cannot applaud their progress.

What is it that assists one client in her efforts toward recovery, but seems not to move another? What is it that helps one client eat . . . but pushes another into more intense starvation (often when out of our view)?

We believe it is, in part, serendipity. If we fall upon the right intervention, the right word, the right metaphor, the right strategy, the right structure for the right or opportune moment in a client's life, then we may view, with great awe, the epiphany . . . the awakening of a life. But if we implement the same strategy, intervention, word, or metaphor at another moment in the client's treatment, we may overwhelm, hurt, or discourage the client in her pursuit of help.

Our timing, tone, words, and approach can determine how effective or ineffective is our intervention.

We have often observed that people with eating disorders need control. Perhaps it is that they, more than most, are unwilling or unable to grant control to others who go against their very nature, timing or appetite. It may be that progress is not seen in the numbers one would expect because clients are being pushed or coerced into a course of treatment that is not of their making. The exception to this rule, however, applies to clients who are medically or psychiatrically at risk. Medical and psychiatric interventions must occur to prolong or save a life, even when the client is precomtemplative and unable or unwilling to recognize the problem or act to save her life. But it is the rare client who indeed meets these criteria of imminent risk. We are now speaking of the majority of clients who feel treatment is either ineffective or, at times, detrimental because the course or content of the treatment does not meet the client where she is.

How can we match the treatment to the client? How can we ensure better, long-lasting outcomes?

We believe the answer is in understanding the stages of change thoroughly researched and scientifically proven by Prochaska and colleagues (Prochaska, Norcross, & DiClemente, 1994). Matching the intervention to the stage of change of the client and working within that stage will help the client move to the next stage. It is the need to trust that the matching and mirroring of the client's timing, or stage, with our intervention, will yield more positive and long-lasting results than the following of a course of treatment that meets some other need, not that of the client.

Although many clinicians are intuitively in touch with their clients' needs, most of us do better by our clients if we are following a structure. Our task is to teach about these stages of change, match the appropriate stage intervention to the client, and move sequentially through the stages with the client. It is, in many ways, like knowing what normal development is for a child, and supporting the child at each step consistent with what that child needs at each step. When we are out of step, or not matching the intervention to the stage of change of our clients we may either be unhelpful or potentially hurtful. When our interventions are timed appropriately, we further the process of development and progress. As an example, when we do not provide a 2-year-old child with the safety and security of our presence, that child might not go off to explore, which is developmentally appropriate. But, when that child feels secure, she will explore readily because she does not have to worry that we'll be there when she is done.

It is our task to provide the safety, security, information, and plan of intervention that will foster each client's efforts at growing the competence and confidence that she can manage her feelings and the world without the eating disorder. This is more likely to occur if we meet the client at her stage of change.

James Prochaska and his colleagues, John Norcross and Carlo DiClemente, set out to understand why some people—those who do and do not seek professional help—either succeed in changing unwanted and problematic behaviors, or do not.

What they found was that most treatment programs, for a large number of problematic behaviors, meet people at the "action" stage of change, yet less than 20% of people who seek treatment are actually at that stage of change. Therefore, excellent programs often fail . . . not because they are not good, but because they are good only for the small segment of the population that is ready to change *now*.

Consequently, many clients blame themselves, the therapist, or facility for no progress. Some leave treatment or experience diminished self-esteem due to the perception that all they do is fail. Many therapists and facilities reinforce this belief by blaming the patient and impugning her motivation.

In Stages of Change theory, it is known, accepted, and understood that most clients who are in treatment, are not ready for change at the action stage. Yet, they may be ready for an intervention at an earlier stage of change.

THE STAGES OF CHANGE

According to Prochaska et al. (1994), there are six stages of change: 1) Precontemplation, 2) Contemplation, 3) Preparation, 4) Action, 5) Maintenance, and 6) Termination. These stages are predictable, follow for all people no matter what problematic behavior they want to change, and are of equal importance in the change process. They have found that matching the intervention to the client's stage of change yields better results than imposing an intervention that does not match the client's stage of change.

We will briefly describe the stages and give examples of stage-appropriate interventions.

Stage 1: Precontemplation

In the Precontemplation stage, the client does not want to be in therapy; she is there under duress. She does not see the symptomatic behaviors as undesirable, or she wishes to maintain the behaviors. Is this not how many clients enter therapy? Many are children who are not allowed to resist therapy. Physicians tell others that they will be hospitalized if they are unable to turn their eating-disordered behavior around.

Often, school personnel or employers tell clients that symptomatic behaviors or physical conditions will interfere with their involvement unless something is done.

In cases like these, education and an emphasis on the pros of change is most effective. Surprisingly, many clients are not educated about their illness and the ramifications of continuing on the same course. They are not given the reasons, concrete and factual, why change is good. These are the clients who, if hospitalized or placed in treatment against their will, will likely go through the motions of change, but revert to old behaviors once discharged or out of the sight of therapists or loved ones.

Stage 2: Contemplation

A client in the Contemplation stage is one who understands the pros of change, but must mourn the loss of the symptoms . . . and thus, the illness. With this client, time must be taken to look at the cons, as well as the pros, of change. How will her life change for the worse? What will she have to give up, do, or feel without this illness? A thorough exploration of these issues and feelings leads to an acceptance of the eating disorder's loss and a moving on.

In treatment, this stage is often overlooked. It is difficult to help a client explore and express reasons why the illness has been good for her, when we see it as nothing but destructive. Yet overlooking the needs of the client at this stage, in an effort to push her into action, often backfires and the client holds more stubbornly to the symptoms that keep her safe.

A young woman and former client, upon trying to understand what led to her recovery after years of severe illness, simply stated, *"patience"* . . . the patience of her therapist . . . which may have led to her eventual readiness to move to the next stage of the change process. Working with clients . . . patiently and compassionately . . . at whatever stage they present, works. Forcing clients into premature action does not.

Stage 3: Preparation

The client in the Preparation stage needs help and rehearsal in preparation for action. This is the stage when the client and therapist identify the goals of behavior change and strategies to reach those goals. This is where they prepare their "war plans" . . . how they will attack and subdue out-of-control behaviors and thinking patterns. This is where they work to secure their environment and bring in as many supports as possible to fortify their efforts.

Most clinicians do well in this stage, but may make the error of pushing action before the plan is fully in place and the client is fully prepared for battle. As in all famous and successful historical battles, foolproof plans secured victory, not impetuous action.

Stage 4: Action

In most treatments and treatment facilities, clinical staff are perched for action. Clients are propelled into action when many are not ready to act. For those who are in the Action stage, the treatment is effective and changing for the good occurs. For those who are not, time and money is wasted, and hope is thwarted.

Action is doing that for which the client is ready and prepared. Action is the active changing of symptomatic behaviors and the trying-on of new, more adaptive behaviors. It is the stage of change that we most value, but as Prochaska and colleagues state, it is no more important in the quest of "Changing for Good" than any other stage. All are important and all must be addressed for successful, long-term change to occur.

Stage 5: Maintenance

In this stage, practice, practice, practice, is the key. Clients need reinforcement to maintain new behaviors and ways of thinking. Usually, the Maintenance stage is one of intense struggle and growing confidence. Here clients will solidify change.

Stage 6: Termination

Clients in this stage have mastered the change. This is when most clients no longer need treatment. They have internalized the skills to maintain the change.

Usually, clients who present for treatment do so in one of the first four stages. We will focus our book on treatment approaches and interventions that are most effective with clients who present in precontemplation, contemplation, preparation, action, and maintenance. We will talk little about the Termination stage, as we, like our primary care physician colleagues, believe that as mental health professionals we must be available to our clients throughout the lifecycle. Although they may no longer need our care for the eating disorder, they need to know we will be available to consult with them should other issues arise in their lives.

We have also seen that our clients may be in different stages of change for different symptomatic behaviors or problems. Matching the intervention to the stage for each symptom or problem will increase the effectiveness of the treatment. For example, a client may not want to change her weight, but she may be ready to stop purging behaviors. We would address these problems with different interventions appropriate to the client's stages of change.

It is our task to present a plan and approach to the treatment of clients with eating disorders, that neither ignores medical and psychiatric sequellae, nor the press of time, while still honoring the client and matching the treatment to her stage of change. Ultimately, matching the intervention to the client's stage of change minimizes the occurrence of medical and psychiatric crises, takes less time over the course of the illness, respects and affirms the patient and her needs, and leads to *Changing for Good*.

The following chart depicts how the stages of change can be applied to the treatment of eating disorders. Under each stage are a list of tasks to accomplish at each stage. Use this chart as a template for determining how to work on eating disorder symptomatology at each stage. The various chapters will go into the tasks associated with each stage in greater detail, especially as they relate to clients' unique situations.

SUMMARY

In this chapter, we reviewed the Stages of Change theory (Prochaska et al., 1994). We looked at some examples of how to apply this theory to our work with clients with eating disorders. If you have worked with clients with eating disorders before, you know that your clients present as unique people with unique problems. Stages of Change theory provides a template for understanding the unique needs of your client so you and she can formulate a plan for change. We have found that our clients engage in the treatment more readily if they have an opportunity to identify their own stages of change. It seems to help them feel more partnership in the process and it fosters intrigue and engagement in the tasks at hand. Perhaps, most importantly, however, this theoretical approach fosters a gentle and patient approach to the client who is not at all ready for change (one in precontemplation stage) as much as it encourages an energetic, action-oriented, problem-solving approach to the client who is ready to change now (action stage). It can soften the harsh judgement of the client against herself (because she is not ready to change now), and it can remind all of us that, in general, our clients are doing the best they can.

*STAGES OF CHANGE AND TASKS: EATING DISORDERS

Precontemplation	Contemplation	Preparation	Action	Maintenance
Eating Disorder ego syntonic and/or client pressured by others	Aware of a problem, but not ready for action	Plans to take action soon & taking small steps	Puts plan into motion; changes behavior/ environment; commitment & energy	Works to prevent relapse & consolidate change; Action successful more than 6 months
Tasks:	_Tasks:_	_Tasks:_	_Tasks:_	_Tasks:_
– Make alliance – Be nonjudgmental – Use questionnaire – Connect ED & consequences – Emphasize pros of change – Get info from others – Educate (e.g. self help, meds, resources, typical tx) – Give medical/nutritional info	– Explore both sides of ambivalence in depth – Generate pros & cons of change for self & others – Keep making connections between ED & consequences – Stress cons of change – Discuss possible treatment plans – Explore difficulties _if_ change occurred – Educate – Consider evocative techniques	– Concretize initial plan for symptom reduction – Define how success & failure will be defined – Define how to monitor – Develop plan B – Review tools: self-help, supports, coping strategies – Reinforce awareness of consequences – Work with others not to enable – Continue to explore difficulties _if_ change occurred	– Mobilize specific tx plan – Work on strategies to cope with feelings, urges, pressures – Review/learn from past relapses – Attend to creeping signs of denial – Consider family/SO work – Explore difficulties _as_ change occurs	– Prevent relapse – Encourage coping skills – Reinforce bond with self-help & other resources – Watch for creeping denial – Encourage new healthy interests – Discuss other life issues as medical/nutritional status improves

* Adapted from: Villapiano, A. (1999) Workshop handouts, Innovative Training Systems, Newton, MA.

The next chapter, Therapist Issues, is meant to encourage those of you who work with clients with eating disorders to reflect upon the issues our clients have raised with us. It also provides questions to ask yourself if you are contemplating working with clients with eating disorders.

The following chapter deals with assessment, and includes self-report forms for the client, family, and significant other. The chapters thereafter deal with issues of: hunger, restrictive eating, binge eating, purging, body image and weight, athletics, substance abuse, and sexual abuse. The final chapters focus on nutritional counseling, medical care, and psychopharmacological issues and management.

In order to protect the confidentiality of our clients, we do not use their real names in the personal vignettes you will read. Much of the identifying data has been changed, as well. Though these changes result in fictional accounts, the feelings, issues, needs, tragedies, and triumphs of these clients are real.

Therapist Issues

Goals:

1. To help therapists understand the concrete and abstract messages they send to their clients through their words, behaviors, and environments.
2. To help therapists determine if and/or how they should work with clients with eating disorders.

How we treat clients with eating disorders is the most important issue, but who treats these clients may be of equally great importance.

Skill, training, and knowledge are essential for all therapists who treat these clients. To understand such psychoeducational material as: the effects of starvation, set point theory, body image, binge eating, purging by various means, low weight, medical abnormalities, and more is essential if one is to understand, inform, and treat these clients.

To have the skill to assess and evaluate these clients and to gather information about thoughts, behaviors, and feelings—shameful or embarrassing, secretive or jealously guarded—is essential, as these clients do not easily divulge that which they see as disgusting or necessary for survival.

It is also essential that the therapist understand cognitive behavioral theory and techniques and have the capacity to develop treatment plans and interventions to reduce binge–purge behaviors, increase eating, decrease body-image distortions, increase socialization, and introduce feared foods.

The following pages discuss issues for therapists to consider before deciding to treat these clients.

THE THERAPIST'S WAITING ROOM

We don't sit and view our waiting rooms as clients do. Our clients with eating disorders have told us what our waiting rooms conveyed to them.

Our waiting rooms were filled with magazines. Most of our clients loved the many choices and enjoyed reading them as they waited for their appointments. Sadly, however, we learned that the magazines toward which they gravitated were the very magazines that reinforced their negative body image and their obsessive focus on food, fat grams, calories, and diets. We also provided newsmagazines, consumer magazines, magazines on gardening, home and architecture, human-interest magazines, and magazines which focused on our city. But they didn't read these. No, they read the fashion, women's, and teen magazines. Just by providing these magazines in our waiting rooms, we were sending our clients the very messages we were trying to eradicate: that the body is an object to be changed and vilified . . . that food is the object of desire and thus, must be tamed and denied . . . and that the women in these magazines are the role models—however unattainable—for our clients to emulate. What were we thinking?

Well, our clients never asked us to remove them, but we felt it was hypocritical of us to promote messages of wellness and empowerment in our therapy sessions if we were "feeding" them propaganda in our waiting rooms.

Although our clients told us that they would choose fashion, women's, and teen magazines first, we decided that in this one space in their lives, we would not support the cultural messages of body dissatisfaction and distortion, food, fat, calorie, or diet obsessions. We cancelled our subscriptions to these magazines and instead, we have tried to find magazines that would support wellness, nourish the mind and spirit, and encourage the possible development of other interests. This was a small step, but significant to our clients and to us.

If waiting rooms are shared, as were ours, this may not always be possible; however, try negotiating with your fellow professionals to see if your waiting room can become a sanctuary for all clients. Like smoking, magazines that promote body dissatisfaction and obsessions with food and fat create a toxic environment. They just happen to be more toxic to our clients, like cigarette smoke happens to be more toxic to an asthmatic. We decided to keep our waiting rooms as toxin-free as we could. And we found it isn't easy!

Waiting rooms sometimes serve as the social and hospitality center, with a bowl of candy, coffee, tea, or cold drinks. Most of us know this is a way we can show caring and hospitality to our clients, but it is good to be aware of the impact food and beverages might have on our clients.

One of our colleagues would often put a bowl of candy in the waiting room to celebrate the holidays. It was a lovely gesture and, I'm sure, appreciated by many clients. For some of our clients with eating disorders, however, it proved to be an overwhelming temptation and a source of anxiety while they waited. It is so hard to meet a lovely gesture with a request to stop. But, we learned that if you share a waiting room with colleagues, requesting that they keep the candy in their own offices to protect your clients with eating disorders from unnecessary stress while waiting, is a reasonable request. Your colleagues will understand as did ours.

A machine serving cold water and hot water for herbal tea is fine for the waiting room. Water needs to be available as a hospitality function and many clients may need it to take their medication or soothe a parched throat. Herbal tea offers warm soothing comfort without adding caffeine, frequently overused by those with eating disorders.

THE THERAPIST'S DRESS

It would be reassuring to think that our clients study their bodies only, but they study ours as well. They have decided quickly if, in their eyes, we are too heavy or too thin, if we hold our bodies with pride or shame, and if we see our bodies as objects to be exposed or hidden.

Through the ways in which we hold, care for, and attire our bodies we can convey respect and admiration for bodies of all sizes and shapes. Sadly, most of us, no matter what our size, are not terribly happy with our bodies. We live in a body-hating society. So be aware. Are you dressing in ways that convey your wish to hide or camouflage your body? Are you dressing in ways that expose or flaunt your body? Try to keep your body messages as neutral as possible. Remember, the focus should be on the client's body issues, not ours. This, of course, is no different than keeping the focus of therapy on the client's content, not ours.

However we attire ourselves, the client may still project her issues upon us. Look for themes from your clients, which may sound something like the following: *Is my therapist hiding her thinness or fatness, as do I? Is he afraid someone will see who he really is, as I am afraid someone will see me? Is she just telling me to eat but she wouldn't/couldn't do the same? He's so good/bad because he's thinner/fatter than I.*

Acknowledging, addressing, and exploring these concerns non-judgmentally and non-defensively is an important step in the therapy process for our clients with eating disorders. Consulting with colleagues has helped us maintain a therapeutic stance with our clients even when our own bodies were being scrutinized. No matter what we think of our bodies, our clients do not deserve to carry our body issues as well as theirs.

THE THERAPIST'S RELATIONSHIP WITH FOOD

It is not uncommon for professionals in this field to have had a history of an eating disorder themselves. The therapist who has struggled with an eating disorder and recovered possesses an invaluable tool in her work with these clients. The therapist who is struggling with an eating disorder herself now, however, does her client and herself a disservice. If you have an eating disorder now, don't work with this population of clients.

If you are a therapist who has recovered from an eating disorder, we suggest that you answer these questions before working with this client population.

1. Is your history something that you will make part of your professional work and identity?
2. If so, what is the benefit to your clients?
3. How would you discern those who could be helped with this knowledge versus those who would use this knowledge to their detriment? For example, one client might feel empowered by this knowledge and see the therapist as a role model for recovery, while another might see it as a sign of the therapist's fragility and become a caretaker.

We suggest that you answer these questions for yourself and review them with a supervisor, consultant, or experienced peer before disclosing your history to your clients.

We strongly urge you to explore and understand your own relationship with food and your body, as your issues may determine how you understand and guide your client.

THE THERAPIST'S USE OF FOOD AND DRINK

If you eat or drink in the therapy session, your client will notice. What are you conveying to your client if during every session you have a can of diet soda on your desk? What are you conveying to your client if you don't take time for lunch but you choose her therapy session to have your lunch? What do you imagine your client thinks when your stomach is growling loudly throughout her session? We think your client is wondering about you. She is wondering *is my therapist a hypocrite telling me not to drink diet soda when she openly consumes it in front of me?* Or she could be wondering how insensitive you are for eating in front of her without asking her to bring her lunch to join you. Or she could be wondering how you could be telling her to take breaks to feed herself when you don't. Finally, your growling stomach could be conveying that you don't eat either.

If your client brings up what she notices, address it non-judgmentally and non-defensively. Ask her what meaning she makes of it. This could lead to a very fruitful discussion.

We have learned that it is best not to eat, or advertise diet beverages, during therapy sessions with our clients. However, it can be tremendously helpful to offer to help your client practice eating with you. We have done this in individual therapy sessions and when we have run partial and evening treatment programs. Clients value having time to practice eating with us. We have seen the benefit of eating the first candy bar with the client who has wanted, but been frightened of, this risk food for months. We have seen how eating breakfast with the client who has never eaten breakfast eased her fear.

Of course, you need to be sure you can eat what your client wants to eat and you need to be sure you can eat appropriately (i.e., normal portion sizes). In other words, don't eat with your clients unless it is done in a planful way for the benefit of the client. It is not acceptable to eat during a therapy hour just because you have not had time for lunch.

If you are seeing many clients with eating disorders who would benefit from practice eating with you, consider starting a meal group. We have found that these groups are very supportive and educational for our clients. There are palpable therapeutic benefits when our clients learn to share their meals and their burdens with others. Sometimes this is the best way to help them learn that meal times are meant to nourish the body and the soul.

CULTURAL AND RELIGIOUS PRACTICES AND ATTITUDES

Ask many questions about your clients' religious and cultural practices and beliefs, especially as they relate to food. Unless you ask questions and feel fully informed, you may inadvertently convey bias or insensitivity. For example, if your client were being raised in a kosher Jewish home, you would not insist that she drink a glass of milk at a meal with meat. If she were raised in a traditional Italian-American home, you would not question if she were binge eating if she had her pasta course and her complete turkey dinner on Thanksgiving.

In our work with clients with eating disorders, we must understand the meaning of food in the client's culture and religion. Although we would choose not to have our anorectic clients fast for certain religious observances, we must be respectful of these observances and look toward the physician or nurse working with this client or family to convey the medical reasons why fasting at this point would be harmful to our client, while still showing respect for the practice of their culture or religion. If a client reports fear of attending a family religious celebration because of the abundance of food served and the pushing of a grandmother or aunt or cousin to feast and enjoy, we might meet with the family to look at ways to help make the meal more manageable for our client. Or, we might request that the client bring in her relatives so we could talk about the food pressures and fears associated with Thanksgiving, Christmas, Passover, Easter, or her cousin's Bat Mitzvah.

If, within a certain culture, eating certain foods or many foods that frighten the client is expected, we might help the client practice eating these foods ahead of time. This exposure and desensitization practice will help the client prepare for the event that often brings interpersonal as well as food-related stresses.

VEGETARIANISM

We recommend that our clients address food issues with a nutritionist who is experienced working with clients with eating disorders. If such a professional is not available in your area, educate yourself about proper nutrition and seek consultation around food and meal planning from the most informed member of your treatment team (e.g., the nurse or physician). The following paragraphs offer a few pointers to therapists working with these clients, especially when doing so without the help of the nutritionist. The final chapter of this book goes into nutritional counseling in greater depth.

Many clients with eating disorders choose to follow a vegetarian diet. Following such a diet does not necessarily indicate that the client is being led there by her eating disorder, but often, it *is* the eating disorder, not a moral or health issue which causes the client to forego animal products. Cutting out animal proteins serves to limit consumption of fats as well as proteins, which is often counterproductive to weight gain, increasing needed iron stores, and building organ and muscle tissue.

Therapists should explore their own beliefs about the issue of vegetarianism. It is imperative not to impose your beliefs about eating onto your client, but instead to help your client learn to feed herself within her belief system until she is ready to expand it. Even if you believe the client's vegetarianism is a weight-loss technique rather than a morally held belief system, work with the client to find the foods, within her vegetarian diet, which she can eat to assure herself adequate sources of protein, fat, and iron. Many clients who follow vegetarian diets cut out red meat, but will eat poultry and fish. Others will only eat fish. Whatever the brand of vegetarianism she follows, your goal will be to help her take care of herself nutritionally and not to do battle with her to get her to eat foods that she either finds morally or physically abhorrent at this time in her life.

It is more difficult to help clients with eating disorders find adequate sources of protein, fat, and iron on a vegan diet, where absolutely no animal products are consumed. If the client follows this diet, encourage her to problem-solve with you as to how to get needed food groups, vitamins, and minerals into her diet when choices are so few. You might ask her to consider allowing certain foods into her diet for their "medicinal" value while she is ill, with the possibility of discontinuing such "medicinal" food choices when she is well.

As with cultural and religious beliefs about food, respect the client's choices of food while working with her to encourage eating what it is she needs within the food choices she feels are available to her. If they are nutritionally deficient, problem-solve with the client how she will get those needed sources of protein, fat, and iron into her diet. A collaborative, problem-solving approach to this dilemma often elicits far better progress with eating goals than forcing or coercion.

THE SEX OF THE THERAPIST

It is not the sex of the therapist, but the training and experience of the therapist, as well as his or her ability to meet each client at her stage of change, which, likely, will determine the therapist's effectiveness with the client. Although some clients expressly request a therapist of a particular sex, it is not the sex of the therapist that determines the therapy's success or failure. As in all issues related to the client, however, the "fit" of the therapist to the client should first be determined by the therapist's skill and training, willingness to work with these clients, and the client's wish to work with this therapist. Female clients who have been sexually abused by a male often request a female therapist and female clients who have concerns about their sexuality often do the same. Otherwise most clients wish only to work with skilled, highly trained therapists.

Male therapists must assess their comfort in asking questions about a client's menses, pregnancies, body-image distortion, and sexual practices before deciding to work with these clients. Like female therapists, male therapists should examine their feelings about body size, weight, and food, and should not work with these clients if they have unresolved issues about their own body size or food practices.

THE PREGNANT THERAPIST

When a therapist is pregnant, she automatically displays the growing physical form found so frightening to clients with eating disorders. To some clients this is overwhelming. For some it is the link between the physical form and sexuality that is overwhelming. To others, it is the longing to be able to nurture another to legitimize nurturing the self that evokes strong feelings. The client with the eating disorder also worries, as do many clients, that the pregnancy will take the therapist away from her, at first figuratively as the therapist turns her attention to her growing fetus, and then, literally as the therapist takes time off after the birth of her baby.

We believe the therapist should tell her clients about her pregnancy before they figure it out. This way she and her clients can predict what issues may come up over her pregnancy and can prepare and strategize to help the client deal with them. Predicting and preparing for changes are skills that all clients need to learn. A therapist's pregnancy offers one more opportunity to work on these skills. Clients sometimes benefit from writing their questions, observations, thoughts, and feelings about the therapist's growing form and baby and how they impact or resonate with her. Reviewing these in the session can be very helpful. Therapists should look for the following issues to surface: (a) the client begins to engage in unprotected sex, (b) the client begins to over or under eat, (c) the client develops "morning sickness," and (d) the client recovers memories of abuse or talks about abortions, miscarriages or pregnancies not talked about before.

THERAPIST/CLIENT "FIT" AND THE USE OF LANGUAGE

Just as some people don't have the right "fit" in other relationships, they may not have the right "fit" with you. Sometimes you'll know it and sometimes you won't. However, if your client is not progressing and you have followed a well-thought-out plan of treatment and addressed openly with your client issues that may be impeding progress, without success, you might want to address the issue of "fit." If the "fit" is wrong, it may be neither yours nor your client's fault, but it will be your fault if treatment continues without progress. Of course, when "fit" is wrong some clients drop out or cancel many times, but others endure because it's what they were taught to do. Some will not tell you it doesn't feel right because nothing has ever felt right and no one has ever asked or cared, so why would you? As the therapist, you must bring it up. This alone has moved an intractably stuck therapy for some. Addressing the issue of "fit" will give the client faith that "what goes on between people" can give rise to problems or can impede health without it necessarily implying blame. (See Chapter 10, Sexual Abuse and Eating Disorders, for approaches to treating clients for whom what went on between themselves and another was truly unacceptable and the fault of the other).

Associated with "fit" is the therapist's ability to accurately assess each client's stage of change and adapt the treatment to fit the needs of that stage. The "fit" in these cases may become appropriate once the therapist changes strategies and focus to mirror the intervention to the client's stage of change.

The therapist's use of pejorative language is often a sign of inappropriate "fit" or failure to offer treatment, which meets the client at her level of change. It is both disrespectful and narcissistic to assume that the reason a client may not be progressing in therapy is the client's "resistance," rather than an inappropriate "fit" or the therapist's incorrect assumption about the client's stage of change, treatment focus, or goals. If you find yourself using pejorative language toward the client, as illustrated by the use of terms such as "resistant," "unmotivated," or "manipulative," seek consultation and review the client's stage of change and your intervention. You might find that by realigning your intervention with the client's stage of change, you'll likely reduce your frustration level and facilitate the client's movement to the next stage.

THE ABUSED CLIENT

According to the research findings of some, there is a strong correlation between eating disorders and a history of abuse. According to that of others, abuse is no more common in the eating disordered population than in the population of those who seek psychiatric care. Because abuse is frequently reported by those who seek psychiatric care and by those who seek treatment for eating disorders, whose statistics you use is moot. Clients who seek treatment for eating disorders may likely have a history of abuse. Therefore, we recommend that therapists with unresolved issues around their own abuse, like therapists with eating disorders, resolve those issues before embarking on treatment with these clients.

Because this topic merits greater depth, we suggest that you refer to Chapter 10, Sexual Abuse and Eating Disorders.

TIME

We make time for that which is important to us. Our use of time shows reverence and respect or disregard and disrespect. Our use of time shows our trustworthiness, consistency, dependability, and efficiency. Our use of time shows that we value the other and ourselves; we neither disregard our time to do more for the other than we can or is needed, nor take from the other her allotted time because we do not plan well enough.

Clients with eating disorders, in our experience, either feel unworthy of anything, including time, or want too much and then feel guilty. As with all clients, it is important to hold sacred your time for these clients, outside of unavoidable emergencies. For example, be prompt. If you are to see a client at 10:00, welcome her in at 10:00, not 10:10. If you need to reschedule, give her as much notice as possible and indicate your regret at having to do so. Start and stop the session on time. Provide your client with a framework she can trust, but do not hold so rigidly to it that emergent human needs cannot be addressed when warranted.

Use time wisely and sparingly. All work must not necessarily be done on the 7-day cycle. Many clients work well, even better, with more space between sessions and clear, structured between-session homework assignments. There are times when a client needs more time. Your ability to be flexible and plan time based more on the client's needs than on a 7-day schedule will encourage and support many clients in their efforts.

THE TREATMENT TEAM

Therapists who choose to work with clients with eating disorders must be willing and welcoming of collaborative efforts between members of the treatment team. The team could consist of a physician or nurse and the therapist only, or it could expand to include a nutritionist, family therapist, psychiatrist, expressive therapist, group therapist, or others. For the client who is hospitalized or being treated at a more intensive level of care, there will be an inpatient, partial hospital, or residential program staff with whom to collaborate. Collaboration takes time and effort. Your client's progress in part depends upon the ability of the treatment team to determine a treatment focus and goals that meet the client at her stage of change. It requires taking the time to share with the members of the treatment team your observations while listening to theirs. A smoothly running treatment team with consistent goals and approaches often facilitates treatment, whereas, the non-collaborative treatment team is likely to introduce iatrogenic problems like those of a dysfunctional family.

If you prefer to work alone on cases or feel unable to make the ancillary time commitment to collaborate with a team of professionals, we recommend that you not treat clients with eating disorders.

THE THERAPEUTIC CONTRACT

Because clients with eating disorders can get into medical jeopardy, a contract that stipulates safe-practice guidelines is essential. This contract must include medical monitoring to assure that the client may be treated safely in an outpatient setting, or efforts to move the client to a more intensive level of care should be initiated. The PCC (primary care clinician; typically a physician, but can be a registered nurse practitioner or physician's assistant) in charge of the client's medical care should, with your input, set safe practice guidelines including: weights, vital signs, and lab results under or over which the client may not be treated safely at the outpatient level of care. It is best if there are a number of medical indicators to be observed because focus on weight alone often reduces all team members and the client to number watching rather than on the more global and complete focus of her general medical condition. (See Chapter 12, Medical Care, for more information.)

Clients with eating disorders all have problems with food; thus, a referral for consultation to a nutritionist experienced in working with clients with eating disorders is essential and supportive of safe-practice guidelines for these clients. (See Chapter 11, Nutritional Counseling, for more information.)

Many clients with eating disorders have comorbid diagnoses such as depression, anxiety disorders, and social phobia. Frequently, these diagnoses can be successfully treated pharmacologically. Additionally, research supports pharmacological intervention to assist in the reduction of binge–purge urges. Thus a referral for consultation to a psychiatrist experienced in working with clients with eating disorders is also essential. Failure to refer for such a consultation early in the treatment episode ignores best practice guidelines for the treatment of clients with eating disorders. For more information on the use of medication and the treatment of co-morbidities, refer to Chapter 13, Pharmacological Issues and Management.

Clients with eating disorders benefit from psychoeducation and goal-focused treatment aimed at reducing eating disordered symptomatology while increasing desired and health-producing behaviors such as normalizing eating, reducing purging, or decreasing practices which reinforce restrictive eating, body-image distortion, and dichotomous thinking.

Collaboratively deciding what you will work on and identifying how you will know if the work that you've chosen to do is helpful naturally constructs the limits, boundaries, and the contract of treatment in a relationally supportive way. This fosters client growth far more than therapist-driven treatment foci or goals does.

As with all other clients, clear guidelines around the scope and limits of your practice, including emergency procedures, calls between sessions, cancellations, vacation coverage, fees, and confidentiality, should be shared with your clients in writing. If you must abide by state or federal laws governing confidentiality or informed consent, share that information with your clients, preferably in writing.

All of this information in addition to a well constructed, collaborative focus for treatment will convey safety, security, and respect to those clients who are unable, at the most basic level, to provide for themselves in ways that insure medical safety, personal security, and respect for body and soul.

CASE LOAD

Clients with eating disorders often present with "weighty" needs and issues. No wonder, whatever their weight, they feel "fat." They are often burdened by real or felt responsibilities for others' happiness, safety, or survival as well as inordinate pressures to do and be perfect in numerous arenas. Furthermore, they may present with medical issues, psychiatric crises, and risky behaviors. These factors combined with the need to plan for ancillary consultation and collaboration time with other treatment providers warrants being careful not to treat so many of such clients that you are shortchanging your clients and yourself by running short of time, energy, or opportunities for rejuvenation. We would suggest treating no more than 20 clients with eating disorders at any one time for the full-time clinician. We recommend far fewer if you are treating many adolescents, those with additional axis I and axis II diagnoses, or those in medical or psychiatric crisis.

INTAKES

Because many of these clients need and warrant greater time and energy commitments from the therapist than others, it is critical to assess the client's needs by phone before agreeing to work with her. If you are already managing as many complicated cases as possible, you do neither the client nor yourself a service by agreeing to see her. It is far better, and more respectful for both the client and yourself, to explain that you will be unable to see the client at this time, but make every effort to refer the client or referent to another therapist you can highly recommend. Making exceptions often leads to frustration and dissatisfaction for therapist and client alike.

SUMMARY

In conclusion, the therapist who works with clients with eating disorders must possess: (a) knowledge of the eating disorders and psychoeducational principles, (b) an ability to work cognitive-behaviorally as well as dynamically and relationally, and (c) clarity and resolution about his or her own body size/weight, food, and abuse issues in order to effectively treat these clients. Furthermore, no therapist should treat these clients alone. Since there are medical sequellae associated with these disorders, therapists should work closely with a physician or nurse, seek a psychopharmacological consultation around the possible use of medications, and consult a registered dietitian for help with meal planning. If you are working with a child or adolescent, it is essential for a family therapist to be part of the treatment team. If possible, all of the professionals should work collaboratively with clients, with the individual therapist coordinating the treatment and keeping in regular consultation with his/her colleagues in order to provide the maximum safety for these patients and the best possible care.

The Initial Assessment

Goals:

1. To help therapists establish an empathic connection with the client.
2. To demonstrate how to gather data and determine the client's stage of change.
3. To teach therapists how to develop a therapeutic plan.

Do you remember the first time you went to a therapist . . . gynecologist . . . dentist . . . surgeon? Do you remember feeling anxious . . . frightened . . . vulnerable . . . confused? Many clients experience these feelings when they first come to you. When you are a patient (or client, as we prefer), you are vulnerable, often scared, anxious, uncertain or confused. You are turning to professionals who have more knowledge and expertise than you do. When you are the one seeking rather than giving the help, you feel the power differential more acutely. You may wonder: Will he/she listen and fully address and respect my questions and fears? Will he/she understand what I need, make recommendations that reflect this understanding, and have the skill to provide what is needed? Will he/she treat me with respect and dignity?

As you think about what made those first experiences seeking professional help beneficial and comfortable versus unhelpful and uncomfortable, you will know what your clients need in their first session.

THE INITIAL GREETING

Greet your client on time, smile, introduce yourself, and shake hands. Wait at the door to your office and gesture where you would like your client to sit. We always sit with our client, across a coffee table, not ensconced behind a desk, which automatically blocks potential for connection. We let our client know that she may feel some anxiety or apprehension in the first meeting, and reassure her that it is normal and expected. Ask if she minds if you take notes. Do make eye contact, even if you are taking notes. More important than notes is your initial connection with the client. She must feel that your entire focus is on her. Note-taking is done to enhance focus, not to distract or block connection.

THE STRUCTURE AND FRAME OF THE SESSION

Let your client know how much time the two of you will have during the session and let her know what you hope to accomplish in the session. For example:

> *We'll have 50 minutes today. I have questions to ask you, and I'm sure you have questions to ask me. My hope is that before you leave here today, we'll understand the problem that brought you here, and have enough information about the problem to decide upon a plan of action.*

If the client has brought you information that she filled out before the session, ask if she would mind if you refer to it during the interview. It conveys how important what she wrote is and assists in making the first session a collaboration.

Save at least 10 to 15 minutes to make your recommendations, making certain that you take into consideration the client's stage of change and the problem as stated by the client. Ask for the client's thoughts about your proposal and decide upon a thinking or writing between-session task, and make an appointment for the next session.

THE FOUR-PART ASSESSMENT

When assessing a client for an eating disorder, gathering information from as many critical sources as possible leads to the most comprehensive and best-formed treatment plan for your client. The sources often missed are the client herself and the family or significant other(s). Clients, of course, are asked to respond to many questions during an interview, but seldom are asked to reflect and respond in writing to questions before or after the initial interview. When a child is seen, we typically request developmental data from the parent, but seldom ask parents, or significant others, to reflect and respond in writing. The combination of the client's, parents', or significant others', and your own assessment data provides for a rich and comprehensive pool of information from which you and your client will fashion the treatment. As well, because time is short, this method of requesting information streamlines the process and often affords the therapist information quickly which can ordinarily take up to 3 sessions or more to gather through direct interview. Finally, many clients and family/significant others feel more comfortable, initially, sharing their thoughts and feelings through writing than through the spoken word.

There are four assessment tools, provided at the end of this chapter. They are the following: the Client Questionnaire, the Parent Questionnaire, the Significant Other Questionnaire, and the therapist's Initial Screening Evaluation.

The Client Questionnaire

The Client Questionnaire is for the client to record her thoughts and feelings concerning her eating disorder, to convey factual information, and to say what she hopes for in the therapy. When the client calls for the initial appointment, ask her if she would be willing to fill out some information for you before the session. If she agrees and there is time, send it to her. If she is willing to have it faxed, fax it to her. Be aware, however, of the sensitive nature of the questions and make sure she understands that faxes cannot be assumed confidential. If the client would prefer, suggest she come to the session a half-hour earlier than her appointment to fill out the questionnaire before the session. If the client hesitates or says she prefers not to do it, let her know it is O.K. and following the first session, if she agrees, she can fill it out.

Some clients need to meet you before they feel comfortable providing you with personal information. Others feel better and more prepared if they have started the process of the evaluation before seeing you. All will know, once seeing the questionnaire, that you are knowledgeable (i.e., that you know what questions to ask), and that you are interested in their observations, thoughts, feelings, and hopes for the therapy. This usually helps them feel more trusting of you, and starts them on a quest for information, which all clients initially need—especially those who are in the stage of Precontemplation.

The Parent Questionnaire

When seeing children and adolescents, it can be difficult to help them feel that the therapy is theirs. It can be extremely difficult to balance the needs of parents and children when you are the child's individual therapist and there is no family therapist involved. Without question, when treating underage children, inclusion of the parents or guardians in family therapy is essential for the child's ability to progress. However, parents often feel excluded, or children feel parents are too included, for the individual therapy to feel affirming and respectful of the child, parents or both. There is no right or wrong way to proceed. Each case should be decided on its individual merits.

Requesting that the parents fill out the questionnaire while the child is being seen for the first session gives the parents something worthwhile to do while waiting and provides them with access to you without shortchanging the child. Greeting the parents warmly and letting them know how important their observations, thoughts, and feelings about their child and the eating disorder are, will reassure them that their input, questions, and concerns will be considered. It is important by the end of the first session that the parents understand your plan for their child, and the parents have someone to meet with soon; if not you, then a family therapist who will collaborate with you.

If you are meeting with a young child under 12, or if you assess that the older child or adolescent is at some risk medically or psychiatrically, meeting with the parents immediately following your initial session with the child is essential to protect the child. In order to maintain the child's/adolescent's trust in you, let them know why you must meet with their parents and what you will say. It is important to ask the child/adolescent if there is anything else he/she would like you to say or not say when the parents come in. If it is possible to respect the child's wishes, do so. If it is not, due to an issue of risk, let the child/adolescent know at that time. Children and adolescents rarely refuse to see a therapist who shares critical information with a parent, with the child's knowledge and in the child's presence. However, to do so without the child knowing or behind the child's back likely will lead to an unproductive therapy, or no therapy at all.

The Significant Other Questionnaire

An adult doesn't need others involved in his or her therapy, as children do. Many adults live alone, are estranged from their families, have isolated themselves from friends, and have secreted themselves behind closed doors with their illness. We are alarmed at the numbers of men and women who have eating disorders who have told no one, including those with whom they live.

We firmly believe that people get better in their natural environments, not in a therapist's office. By this we mean that although our client may learn a great deal and benefit inordinately from our work together, unless there is at least one other person in her life who knows about the eating disorder and has been involved in learning how to support recovery, the client will have more difficulty progressing. Thus, the Significant Other Questionnaire is our way to bring in an outside support for our client. We believe that including a range of significant others can quickly widen the client's network of support, thus reducing the client's isolation with the illness. Should no significant others exist for a client, immediately hook her up with the self-help support network in your area. We recommended this for all clients, but particularly those who are alone.

The significant other could be a spouse, partner, lover, roommate, friend, or relative. It's best if it is a person who knows the client well, but if that's not possible, consider whomever the client believes could/would care enough to be included. The significant other, like the parent of the child or adolescent, is asked to offer his or her observations, thoughts, and feelings about the eating disorder. This breaks the code of secrecy and silence and allows the client more potential support in her efforts at recovery from the eating disorder.

Finally, gathering all this data in writing is both an effective use of time and resources. In traditional therapies, it could take many sessions to gather such information in face-to-face meetings.

The Initial Screening Evaluation

In the initial screening the most important question to ask the client is, *Why now?* Why is the client seeking therapy now? Is someone else demanding it? Has there been some medical, psychiatric, relationship, work, or educational crisis? Is the client on her own feeling the press of time, age, mortality, or position in life? Has the client come to this decision, not from crisis or pressure, but from planfully attempting to work on her issues without the success she desires?

Whatever the reason, it is important to know, as it will often tell you at what stage of change the client enters your office. For example, "I'm here because my doctor won't let me compete on the swim team until my weight and vital signs are more stable, but I don't think I have a problem" represents quite a different stage from the client who says, "I'm here because I've been working hard to reduce my purging behavior over the past 6 months, and although I'm not vomiting at work anymore, I can't seem to stop it at night when I'm home. I really want to stop the vomiting at night!"

Asking "Why now?" will tell you what your client wants and needs and what others in her environment might be wanting or needing. It tells you where to start. With the first client, stage 1, Precontemplation, is her stage. She is being coerced into treatment. She might not know how the eating disorder will eventually impact on her ability to swim competitively. Psychoeducational information is essential for this client while inquiring of her what she imagines it would be like if her eating disorder were not putting her at such risk. Such questions might help her to move into stage 2, Comtemplation, more quickly. For the second client, Action, the 4th stage, is her stage. She has already been taking action to stop purging during the day, but, for whatever reasons, her daytime plan is not working at night. You and she might have to move back to the stage of Preparation to plan for how to attack this problem at night before she can move back into Action.

Much of the Initial Screening Evaluation follows that of generic screening tools but adds the essential questions around the client's use and abuse of food, purgatives, and her body while attempting to ascertain how these interfere with her life. Finally, it helps you determine your client's stage of change regarding several possible problematic behaviors. For example, a client may be at the Precontemplation stage around weight gain, but at the Contemplation stage around increasing her intake of proteins and dairy foods. You might try to educate her about the concept of "set point" so she understands body weight issues, and provide her with articles to read concerning female athletes, competition, and body weight. Around the issue of her intake of protein and dairy foods, in addition to providing her with information, you might puzzle with her how it might change her life for the worse, as well as the better, if she starts to consume more proteins and dairy. Clients often do well when writing the pros and cons for changing and not changing, so they can visually see both sides. Often this leads clients to underlying issues such as that voiced by this client:

> *If I eat more protein and dairy, and if I gain weight, my father will go back to working day and night, and I'll never see him because he'll think I'm all better. I hate to say it, but being sick was the only way I knew my father loved me.*

When the client hears that you understand how important the eating disorder has been for her because it led her to the belief that her father truly loved her, she will likely feel affirmed in her jealous guarding of the illness, which will help her begin to let it go. This respect for the symptom and the role it has played helps clients confront their ambivalence, weaken the illness' hold, mourn the potential loss of the symptom, and eventually work toward considering other less destructive ways of coping with feelings and needs. This sequence naturally moves them to the stage of Preparation. With your help, she will begin to "prepare" how to bring this insight and issue to her father. Catalyzed by the question, *Why now?* a client can move from Contemplation to Preparation in the initial screening session.

EARLY STAGES OF CHANGE

Should your client arrive in stage 1, Precontemplation, remember to give information. Although information and education are the only things a client at this stage can take in, they can be very powerful agents of change for some. Send her out with things to read: copies of articles, pamphlets, or other handouts. Request that she do a *thinking* task in an effort to see if she can move to the next stage. For example, "What do you think it would be like to go a day without vomiting? What do you think it would be like to concentrate through an entire class? What do you think it would be like to go to bed without your stomach growling with hunger?"

If your client arrives in the stage of Contemplation, stage 2, she knows all the reasons to change but has not yet imagined life without the help that the symptoms provide. She needs to understand how the symptoms "helped" her followed by a mourning of their loss. Only if you and she pay homage to the symptom, acknowledging what it did for her, will she be able to let it go. She must fully understand why she needed the symptom, to embrace all the reasons why she now must let it go. Asking questions such as:

> *What does the vomiting do for you? How has it helped you? What will life be like without the vomiting when you are afraid, lonely, and angry . . . ? How does it help you to go days without food? What will it be like when your empty stomach no longer numbs the pain . . . anxiety . . . loneliness . . . fear?*

Such questions will help her to move through this stage of change.

ENDING THE INITIAL EVALUATION SESSION

Clients do best with a succinct summary of the therapy session followed by a proposed plan. The plan must address the problem *as the client sees it*, not as others see it. For example, in the scenario above of the girl who could not compete on the swim team due to her restrictive eating, low weight, and vital signs, she is not saying, *"I have an eating disorder and I want help."* She is, however, implying that she wants to compete on the swim team, regardless of her condition.

In summarizing her session and conveying a plan, the following might capture her desire, without neglecting her physician's concerns, and while meeting her at her stage of change:

> *You have said that your doctor won't allow you to compete until your weight and vital signs are stable. It is clear to me that you want to compete because you're here; but it's also clear to me that your eating disorder helped you feel something important that you did not feel before . . . and that is your father's love. So you have the eating disorder which has caused you to eat restrictively, lose weight, develop unstable vital signs, and lose the ability to compete . . . while helping you feel loved by your father. I see that you are facing a terrible dilemma . . . the eating disorder gives, but it takes . . . to get what it gives, you must give up what it takes. It seems there is quite a decision to make.*
>
> *I would suggest two things that might help us understand this dilemma better. The first is to write down all that the eating disorder has taken and all that it has given to you. You've certainly mentioned some important things here, but I wonder if there are more. Next, I would ask you to think about what it would be like to eat more protein and dairy. It might weaken the eating disorder. What would that be like for you? Again, you've mentioned something very important here today . . . that your father might think you're well and not show his love for you. But I wonder if there are other things that you imagine might change as a result of eating more protein and dairy?*
>
> *If you would think about these two questions (and, if you're up to it, write down your thoughts) I think it would help us figure out how you could both compete on the swim team and keep your father's love, because you've made it clear that you want both.*

This summary respects the client's wishes and goals, supports the physician's goals, and meets the client at her stage of change. Furthermore, it honors her struggle, affirms that the therapist understands, makes clear that we will work collaboratively, and provides hope that we may be able to find a way for her to have what she wants. Finally, my request for her to think and write before our next session furthers the work of the session, offers her ownership of the work, and may help galvanize her commitment to change.

THE CONSULTATION

For clients whom you are seeing in consultation with another therapist or for a second opinion, the format for the initial evaluation will be the same except you will be requesting the observations, thoughts, feelings, questions, and goals of the other therapist. When summarizing the session, it is also important to convey a plan for how the client will continue this work with her therapist.

Of course, as in all cases where clients have a current therapist, or past history of treatment, requesting to have releases signed so you may consult with these treatment providers is essential. If the request for the consultation comes from the therapist, with the client's permission, speak with the therapist first. If the client is requesting the consultation, speak with the client first. It is very important that you make clear that you are the consultant and, thus, you will not be available to see the client beyond the consultation.

During the initial assessment, the therapist should be aware of the multitude of feelings the client may be experiencing. Vulnerability, anxiety, and other difficult feelings can significantly hinder the client's pursuit for recovery. For these reasons, the initial assessment is critical; the more comfortable the client feels in the first session, the more likely she is to continue in treatment. It is the job of the therapist to make the client feel as comfortable as possible, while collecting pertinent information.

Gathering information from family and significant others can further enhance the assessment process. The tools in this chapter will help the therapist conduct a comprehensive assessment for those seeking treatment for an eating disorder.

SUMMARY

Clients should leave your office after the initial screening evaluation with a clear understanding of the plan. If they are to return to you, they have heard from you what you think should be the focus of the treatment. They will have had the time to discuss this with you, and you and they will have decided upon a between-session thinking or writing task.

If you feel a referral to another professional is warranted, for nutritional, psychopharmacological, medical, family, or group work, you should provide your client with a name and phone number. If you are not certain of a colleague's availability or willingness to see a particular client, you should call that colleague ahead of time to make certain the client is not making calls to professionals who are not available.

As clients need networks of support, providing names and phone numbers of support groups in your area and targeting for your client the ones that might be most helpful to her is essential. For those who are alone, this may be their only support outside of you. For those who will have difficulty approaching family or friends, this will be a haven until they are able to do so.

If the initial evaluation session is successful, the client will leave believing there is hope.

> I am not "crazy" for wanting/needing this illness at this time. I will not have to be alone with this forever; Someone understands; and, there may be a way for me to get what I want and need without losing the only thing(s) that I think I have right now.

CLIENT QUESTIONAIRE

Name: _____ Today's Date: _____

Address: _____ Phone: _____

_____ D.O.B. _____

Marital Status: Single ___ Married ___ Separated ___ Divorced ___ Widowed ___

Current living arrangements: With parents and/or relatives ___ Dorm or with friends ___
with partner/spouse ___ alone ___

Current Weight: _____ lbs. Height: _____

Family Weight History:
   Is your mother currently living (Y/N)? _____ Mother's age: _____
   Describe Mother's weight (check one):
     severely underweight _____ underweight _____ average weight _____
     slightly overweight _____ overweight _____ severely overweight _____

   Is your father currently living (Y/N)? _____ Father's age: _____
   Describe Father's weight (check one):
     severely underweight _____ underweight _____ average weight _____
     slightly overweight _____ overweight _____ severely overweight _____

   Number of siblings and names:
   _____

   How many siblings are overweight? _____ Underweight? _____

   Does anyone in your family have a history of dieting and/or pre-occupation with food/weight? Please explain.
   _____
   _____
   _____
   _____
   _____

Body Image History:
   Please indicate how satisfied you feel with the way your body is proportioned:
    very dissatisfied _____ dissatisfied _____ slightly satisfied _____ satisfied _____ very satisfied _____
   Please indicate how you feel about the different areas of your body:
    VD= very dissatisfied D=dissatisfied SS=slightly satisfied S=satisfied VS=very satisfied

    Face: _____ Arms: _____ Shoulders: _____ Breasts: _____
    Stomach: _____ Buttocks: _____ Thighs: _____ Legs: _____
    Nose: _____ Eyes: _____ Ears: _____ Hair: _____

Please indicate how you see yourself when you look in the mirror?

emaciated _____ thin _____ average _____ slightly overweight _____ overweight _____ extremely overweight _____

Food History:

Please record a sample of your daily intake (food and liquid). Please indicate with a "P" the times in which food/liquid was purged.

Breakfast:

_____
_____
_____
_____

Snack:

_____
_____
_____
_____

Lunch:

_____
_____
_____
_____

Snack:

_____
_____
_____
_____

Dinner:

_____
_____
_____
_____

Snack:

_____
_____
_____
_____

How comfortable are you with your current food behaviors?
Not at all uncomfortable _____ slightly uncomfortable _____ uncomfortable _____
very uncomfortable _____ extremely uncomfortable _____

How ready do you feel to let go of the thoughts/behaviors associated with the eating disorder?
Not at all ready_____ slightly ready _____ ready _____ very ready _____

Please elaborate on reasons why you checked the above box:
_____
_____
_____
_____
_____

How willing would you be to gain 5–10 pounds if you knew the behaviors/thoughts would diminish?
Not at all willing _____ somewhat willing _____ willing _____ very willing _____

Please list the behaviors/thoughts that you would want to change:
_____   _____
_____   _____
_____   _____
_____   _____
_____   _____

At what age did you first become concerned with your weight? _____
At what age did you begin restricting your intake? _____
At what age did you begin purging? _____
At what age did you begin bingeing? _____

Please check all the symptoms you have felt since the development of your eating problems:
Sore throat _____ Feeling tired/weak _____ Feeling bloated _____
Constipation _____ Stomach pains _____ Feeling cold _____
Dizziness _____ Swollen glands _____ Sore joints _____
Water retention _____ Hair loss _____ Muscle spasms/cramps _____
Oversensitivity to noise/touch /light _____ Depression/irritability _____
other (explain): _____

If you have a history of bingeing, please answer the following:
Please check the times you are most likely to binge:
8–12 a.m. _____ 12–6 p.m. _____ 6 p.m.–midnight _____ midnight–8 a.m. _____
Please check the places that you are most apt to binge:
car _____ home _____ work/school _____ restaurant _____ other(explain):_____

Feelings History:

Please place a check next to the feelings that you have difficulty sitting with and/or expressing (that may then get expressed/released through your eating disorder):

Anxiety _____ Boredom _____ Disappointment _____
Confusion _____ Anger _____ Frustration _____ Sadness _____
Fear _____ Guilt _____ Hurt _____ Jealousy _____ Self-loathing _____

Exercise History:

How many minutes per day do you currently exercise? _____

How many days per week do you currently exercise? _____

Are you, or have you ever, been involved in serious training for any sport (Y/N)? _____

If Yes, please list those sports: _____

Sexual History:

Have you ever engaged in sexual intercourse (Y/N)? _____

Has anyone ever touched you in a way that felt uncomfortable, or forced you to participate in a sexual act against your will (Y/N)? _____

Questions:

What are some questions that you would like to have addressed in your next therapy session:

_____
_____
_____
_____
_____

What are some questions that you would like to have addressed in the course of your therapy:

_____
_____
_____
_____
_____

PARENT QUESTIONNAIRE

Name: _____ Education Level:_____

Date of Birth: _____ Marital Status: _____

Occupation: _____ Children (Names and ages): _____

Child's Name: _____

When did you first notice your child was having difficulties with an eating disorder?

_____

_____

_____

_____

_____

Please describe the eating-disordered behaviors you have witnessed and/or suspected with your child. Please differentiate between what you have actually seen from what you suspect or have heard from others.

_____

_____

_____

_____

_____

Have you spoken with your child regarding your concerns? If so, how has your child reacted? If you have not spoken, why?

_____

_____

_____

_____

_____

Have others approached you with concerns for your child? If "Yes," please list those people, and state their concerns (as stated to you):

_____

_____

_____

_____

_____

What impact, if any, has your child's eating disorder had on your current family system? Have you noticed changes within the family system either prior to, or since, the development of your child's eating issues?

_____

_____

_____

_____

_____

In your opinion, why do you believe your child has developed an eating disorder? (Please check all those that apply):

teasing about appearance _____ problems at school/work _____ media influences _____

conflicts between you and your spouse _____ conflicts between siblings _____

conflicts between you/your spouse, and your child _____ puberty and assoc. changes _____

medical reasons (illness/operation) _____ depression _____ loss/divorce _____

difficulty coping with stresses(s) _____ obsessive/compulsive tendencies _____

relational issues with friends _____ leaving home/separation _____ issues with sexuality _____

difficult sexual experience _____ family difficulties _____ prolonged period of dieting _____

recommendation of weight loss by parent, physician, coach, other _____

other reason (please state): _____

_____

Please describe the relationship you have with your child:

_____
_____
_____
_____
_____

Please describe the relationship your child has with your spouse/partner:

_____
_____
_____
_____
_____

Please describe the relationship your child has with his/her siblings:

_____
_____
_____
_____
_____

Whose initiative was it to seek out treatment for your child?

_____
_____
_____
_____
_____

How willing are you to become involved in your child's treatment (including family therapy):

Very willing _____ Somewhat willing _____ Not at all willing _____

Please describe your child's developmental milestones, as well as strengths and weaknesses (socially, academically, physically, emotionally):

_____

_____

_____

_____

_____

Were there other stresses, losses, or difficult experiences that coincided with your child's development of an eating disorder?_____ If so, please describe:

_____

_____

_____

_____

_____

Family History: Please check and note number and relationship of first degree relatives that have experienced the following:

Illness	Number of persons	Relationship to child
Ulcers	_____	_____
Colitis	_____	_____
Asthma	_____	_____
Anxiety	_____	_____
Depression	_____	_____
Manic Depression (Bipolar Disorder)	_____	_____
Alcoholism	_____	_____
Drug Addiction	_____	_____
Anorexia Nervosa	_____	_____
Bulimia	_____	_____
Compulsive Eating	_____	_____
Obesity	_____	_____
Diabetes	_____	_____
Obsessive Compulsive Disorder	_____	_____
Learning Disorders	_____	_____
Suicide Attempts	_____	_____

Please list any questions you would like addressed concerning your child and treatment planning (as well as questions you have regarding eating disorders):

_____

_____

_____

_____

_____

SIGNIFICANT OTHER QUESTIONNAIRE

Name: _____

Date of Birth: _____

Occupation: _____

Spouse's Name: _____

When did you first notice your significant other was having difficulties with an eating disorder?

_____

_____

_____

_____

_____

Please describe the eating-disordered behaviors you have witnessed and/or suspected with your significant other. Please differentiate between what you have actually seen from what you suspect and/or have heard from others.

_____

_____

_____

_____

_____

Have you spoken with your significant other regarding your concerns? If so, how has he/she reacted? If you have not spoken to your significant other, why?

_____

_____

_____

_____

_____

Have others approached you with concerns for your significant other? If "Yes," who is concerned and why?:

_____

_____

_____

_____

_____

What impact, if any, has your significant other's eating disorder had on your relationship? Have you noticed changes within the relationship/ family system/roommate system either prior to, or since, the development of your significant other's eating issues?

_____

_____

_____

_____

_____

In your opinion, why do you believe your significant other has developed struggles with an eating disorder? (Please check all those that apply):

teasing about appearance _____ problems at school/work _____ media influences _____

conflicts between you and your significant other _____ conflicts between siblings _____

conflicts between parents _____ puberty and assoc. changes _____

medical reasons (illness/operation) _____ depression _____ loss/divorce _____

difficulty coping with stressor(s) _____ obsessive/compulsive tendencies _____

relational issues with friends _____ leaving home/separation _____ issues with sexuality _____

difficult sexual experience _____ family difficulties _____ prolonged period of dieting _____

recommendation of weight loss by parent, significant other and/or physician _____

other reason (please state):

_____

_____

Please describe the relationship you have with your significant other:

_____

_____

_____

_____

_____

Who's initiative was it to seek out treatment for your significant other?

_____

_____

_____

_____

_____

How willing are you to become involved in your significant other's treatment:

Very willing _____ Somewhat willing _____ Not at all willing _____

Please describe your significant other's strengths and weaknesses:

_____

_____

_____

_____

_____

Are there other stresses/changes/losses that you think contributed to your significant other's eating disorder?_____
If so, please describe:

_____

_____

_____

_____

_____

Please list any questions you would like addressed concerning your significant other's treatment (as well as questions you have regarding eating disorders):

_____

_____

_____

_____

_____

INITIAL SCREENING EVALUATION

Today's Date: _____

Name: _____   Physician's Name: _____

Address: _____   Address: _____

_____

_____

Phone: (   ) _____   (home) Phone: (   ) _____

(   ) _____   (work)

Date of birth: _____   Insurance: _____

I.D. Number: _____

Emergency Contact: _____   Authorization: _____

Phone Number: (   ) _____

Marital Status: _____

Why Now? (Why is the client coming for help now?)

_____

_____

_____

_____

_____

Presenting Problem (in client's words):

_____

_____

_____

_____

_____

Treatment History:

Please list treatment providers/facilities, and dates of treatment. What was it about each treatment that helped (in client's own words):

_____

_____

_____

_____

_____

Medical History (including dates of illnesses/injuries/surgeries):

_____   _____   _____

_____   _____   _____

Date of last physical exam: _____

Current Medications:

_____

_____

Weight History: Current Weight_____ Highest Weight_____

           Lowest Weight_____ Desired Weight _____ Height _____

Food History:

     Restrictive Eating (please check all those that apply):

         skipping meals _____ reducing portions _____ dieting _____ fasting _____

         reducing calories _____ restricting carbohydrates _____ restricting fats _____

         restricting protein _____ restricting dairy _____ other (explain) :

         _____

         _____

     Purging Behaviors (including numbers and frequency):

         Laxatives: _____   Diet Pills: _____

         Vomiting: _____   Exercise: _____

         Suppositories: _____   Enemas: _____

         Diuretics: _____   Ipecac Syrup: _____

     Bingeing Behaviors (please check all those that apply):

         overeating sweets _____ overeating carbohydrates _____ overeating dairy products _____

         feeling out of control when eating _____ overeating in a period of two hours or less _____

         feelings of guilt/shame after eating _____ eating until physically uncomfortable _____

         other (explain):

         _____

         _____

History of Scale: How often does client weigh self? _____

     Is there a correlation between use of scale and intake and/or purging behaviors? _____

     If "Yes," please describe:

     _____

     _____

     _____

     _____

Menstruation History: Is client currently menstruating (Y/N)_____

     If "No," weight at which menstruation stopped: _____

     If "Yes," is menstruation regular or irregular: _____

Onset of Illness:

(In client's words) How do you think the eating disorder began?

_____

_____

_____

_____

Possible precipitants to the development of the eating disorder, or events that coincided with the development of the eating disorder (please check all those that apply):

teasing about appearance _____ problems at school/work _____ media influences _____

conflicts between you and family member(s) _____ puberty and assoc. changes _____

medical reasons (illness/operation) _____ depression _____ death/loss _____

divorce _____ difficulty coping with stress _____ obsessive/compulsive tendencies _____

relational issues with friends _____ leaving home/separation _____ family difficulties _____

difficult sexual experience _____ prolonged period of dieting _____ issues with sexuality _____

recommendation of weight loss by parent, physician, coach, other _____

other reason (please state)

_____

_____

_____

_____

_____

Family History: (include family history of medical, psychiatric, addiction issues):

(Genogram):

In one sentence describe your

Relationship with your Mother:

_____

_____

Relationship with your Father:

_____

_____

Relationship with your siblings:

_____

_____

Relationship with your spouse/partner/significant other (if applicable):

_____

_____

Current living arrangements:

_____

Religion/Ethnicity:

_____

Legal Concerns (including shoplifting, gambling, etc.):

_____

_____

_____

_____

_____

Trauma History:

   Has anyone ever touched you in a way that hurt? (If so, whom, and when)

_____

_____

_____

_____

_____

   Has anyone ever touched you in a way that made you feel uncomfortable? (If so, whom, and when)

_____

_____

_____

_____

_____

   Has anyone ever said things to you that hurt your feelings (verbally/emotionally)? (If so, by whom, and when)

_____

_____

_____

_____

_____

   Have you ever witnessed any forms of abuse? (If so, by whom, and when)

_____

_____

_____

_____

_____

Substance Use/Abuse History:

Have you ever used alcohol to help induce purging behaviors?

_____

_____

_____

_____

_____

Have you ever taken any drugs/medications to help facilitate food restriction?

_____

_____

_____

_____

_____

Do you turn to substances to help find relief from painful feelings?

_____

_____

_____

_____

_____

If yes, please describe substances used, frequency, and associated consequences:

_____

_____

_____

_____

_____

Sleep History:

Do you ever binge and/or purge in order to fall asleep at night?

_____

_____

_____

_____

Do you ever wake up in the middle of the night, and find yourself bingeing and/or purging?

_____

_____

_____

_____

If you do wake up in the middle of the night is there a pattern regarding either the time waking up, and/or number of hours slept before awakening? (please explain)

_____

_____

_____

_____

_____

Suicide History:

Do you ever intentionally hurt yourself (e.g. cutting, burning, hitting)?

_____

_____

_____

_____

_____

Do you have a history of suicide attempts?

_____

_____

_____

_____

_____

Are your gestures/attempts associated with the use of food and/or purging?

_____

_____

_____

_____

_____

Other Psychosocial Stresses:

What else is going on that hasn't been asked, or is there anything more that you would like to share that would be helpful to add?

_____

_____

_____

_____

_____

Mental Status Exam:

Appearance:

___Neat ___Well Groomed ___Casual Dress ___ Unkempt

Behavior:

___ Calm ___Restless ___Agitated ___Psychomotor retardation ___Suspicious

Level of Consciousness:

___Alert ___Confused ___Delirious

Orientation:

___Person ___Place ___Time

Attention:

___Normal ___Distractible ___Variable

Memory:

___Intact ___Impaired recall ___Impaired recognition

Mood:

___Euthymic ___Depressed ___Angry ___Elated ___Irritable ___Hostile

Affect:

___Appropriate ___Inappropriate

Speech:

___Normal rate and rhythm ___Rapid ___Slow ___Loud ___Soft

Thought Process:

___Coherent ___Goal directed ___Tangential ___Disorganized

Judgement:

___Unimpaired ___Impaired

Insight:

___Unimpaired ___Impaired

Diagnosis:

Axis I: _____

Axis II: _____

Axis III: _____

Axis IV: _____

Axis V: (within past year): Highest GAF: _____ Lowest GAF: _____ Current GAF: _____

Treatment Assessment:

Precontemplation Stage: Denial or unwillingness to accept problem

Contemplation Stage: Know of problem; fear of change—unprepared for change

Preparation Stage: Not knowing how/what to do to change

Action Stage: Implementing change; readiness and learning

Maintenance Stage: Action with increased ease toward change

Please describe the stage of change client presents in with regard to the following:

Purging: _____

Restricting: _____

Binge eating: _____

Low Weight: _____

Body Image Distortion: _____

Treatment Recommendations (please circle those that apply):

Level of care: Inpatient Psychiatric   Inpatient Medical   Partial Hospitalization

Outpatient Intensive (explain): _____

Outpatient Moderate (explain): _____

Outpatient Infrequent (explain): _____

Referrals: (Name and phone numbers)

Nutritionist: _____

Psychopharmacologist: _____

Family therapist: _____

Support Groups (circle):

    ACOA   Alanon   Alateen   A.A.   N.A.   Eating Disorder Group

    Other: _____

Stage of change:

    Precontemplation: Education, Pros of change

    Contemplation: Cons of change

    Preparation: Explore alternatives/Coping strategies

    Action: Implementation

Please explain stage of change and plan:

_____

_____

_____

_____

_____

Homework given:

_____

_____   _____

Clinician's signature and discipline   Date

Understanding Hunger

Goal

To teach therapists how to identify, differentiate, and fulfill physical, emotional, social, and cultural hungers.

Hunger: a strong urgency or desire for food. During infancy until about age 3, the concept of hunger is quite clear. The child feels the physical signs of hunger and cries or asks for food. This is called demand feeding. That is, the child will request food and eat until physically satisfied; once physically satisfied, the child will turn away any food. She is very much aware of her physical needs for food. She has no cognitive understanding of eating for emotional and/or social reasons. Unfortunately, this ability to de-mand-feed appears to dissipate around age four. By this time many children have been taught to use food as a source of comfort, a means of control, and a source of emotional sustenance. As you will see in the example below, many of us have a tendency to teach children to deal with their emotional needs and hungers through food.

> Four year old Kelly is at a playground with her mother and many of her friends. She is playing on the swing set, when she loses her balance and falls off the swing. Her mother comes running over to her and Kelly rushes to Mom's arms. Her knee is scraped and bleeding. Kelly looks down at her bleeding knee and begins to cry harder. Mom knows that Kelly is okay, and wants to help Kelly settle down. Unfortu-nately, her soothing voice and hug is not enough for Kelly, who is still overwhelmed by her bloody knee. Finally, in exasperation, Kelly's mom offers to buy Kelly some ice cream; Kelly stops crying. The ice cream has taken Kelly's focus off of her bloody knee, which leaves her mom feeling successful in helping Kelly through this painful experience. However, subconsciously, Kelly is learning that food can make her feel better, as it did in this episode.

Her mother's innocent act, especially if it is repeated every time Kelly is upset, will teach Kelly that food assuages emotional pain and fear. She will learn to satisfy her emotional needs with food rather than emotional sustenance. No matter how much food Kelly is offered, she may experience a growing emotional hunger because food can never fill her emotional needs. Because she does not know how to fill her emotional needs she will continually go back to food. Over time food may be used to fill all emotional needs such as loneliness, boredom, depression, or sadness, not just the pain and fear it was used to extinguish initially. We can learn to use food to dull our pain.

We can learn to use food to reward accomplishments and we can deny food to punish failure. For example, every time Kelly is "good" (e.g., she urinates in the toilet instead of her bed) she is given a chocolate bar. Otherwise, she never gets a chocolate bar. In time, Kelly will learn that the only time she can have a chocolate bar is when she is "good." The adult version of this is, "I'm overweight; therefore, I can't have a piece of cake. If I were 'good' I would deserve cake." Not only do we learn to deny, avoid, assuage, and mollify feelings with food, but also we learn to use or avoid food to define ourselves as "good" or "bad."

In all of these examples, emotional needs and hungers are satisfied or punished with food. We serve our clients well by plumbing the depths of their emotional hungers and needs. Maybe we can help them make food just food.

When food is just food, it fulfills its physiological purpose, and, with ease and comfort, it can be the way we mark a special event, a gathering, or a celebration. When food is just food, we can share in special occasions and celebratory events without overindulging or restricting.

For example, we serve special meals at special events. We bake and eat birthday cakes to celebrate birthdays. We buy chocolates for people we love on Valentine's Day. We are a society, as are most societies, which celebrates and marks special events with food. Jane Hirschmann and Carol Munter (1988) write extensively about demand feeding as a way to prevent overeating in children and adults. They ask us to go back to how we were with food before the age of four. A four-year-old would not choose food to bury an emotional hurt, nor would she refuse a piece of birthday cake to punish herself for feeling emotional pain or to signify that she is "not good." Somehow, food has become our society's Band-Aid and stick. It soothes and it punishes. Hirschman and Munter try to teach us that food is just food. Eat it when you want it. Eat what you want. Learn to honor and feed yourself with food when you need food, with care when you need care, and with friends when you need friends.

We all have emotional hungers. Those with eating disorders attempt to obliterate, stuff down, or starve away these hungers. The client with anorexia will deny emotional needs through denial of food. Denying this "emptiness," to the anorexic, feels better than acknowledging that such an emptiness exists. Is it not safer to deny a hunger than to acknowledge that it is too "big" to fill? Not only is she fearful of becoming too "big" physically, but she is frightened of how big is her emotional void. Others acknowledge their emotional needs, but feel undeserving of emotional and, thus, physical sustenance.

The client with bulimia, or binge-eating disorder, expresses her emotional hunger through her voracious intake of food. To satisfy this "hunger," she eats, but the "hunger" is never assuaged. Then, overcome with guilt and shame, she purges to expel the food/feelings or sleeps to "escape" the pain.

To punish herself for her needs and/or her indulgence, she uses food or restricts food as her weapon. She may use or avoid food to self-destruct. Or she may use or avoid food to protect. Food can be a weapon of destruction, a protection, or both.

Holidays . . . family gatherings . . . socializing with friends. Most often these events, and others, go hand in hand with food. It is not uncommon to get together with friends over dinner. Most of us look forward to eating a hot dog at a sporting event. At cocktail parties we eat while we socialize, even when we're not really very physically hungry. This is normal; where there is socialization, there is food.

Social hunger is when we eat not because we are physically hungry or emotionally hungry, but because others are eating and food is "there." People with an eating disorder cannot eat in public even when the occasion calls for eating. They feel they always need a reason to eat. Usually, the only acceptable reason is because someone in authority (e.g., physician, nutritionist) tells them they must or when they are truly famished and "safe" food is available. Anything else feels illicit. Part of recovery includes learning to comfortably eat in public. Learning to celebrate or socialize with food without over- or underindulgence is a skill most people benefit from learning.

The final issue we will address is our society's "hunger" for healthy eating, which has come to mean "fat free" eating.

In our era of "fat free" foods, society has emotionally labeled foods as "good" and "bad." Having a piece of chocolate cake, for example, is "bad"; yet snacking on a piece of fruit, or fat free cookies is "good." There has been a fine line developed between healthy eating and unhealthy eating. Unfortunately, those with eating disorders often cross the line without awareness. What can start out as healthy eating can quickly become very rigid and obsessional, and can lead to the development of an eating disorder.

Carolyn is an 18-year-old college freshman who gained approximately 10 pounds within her first three months of college. During her Christmas break, Carolyn decided to go on a diet. She began by incorporating healthy snacks into her daily schedule, which mostly consisted of fruits and vegetables. She also decided to stay away from fast foods, which were commonplace at school. These two changes caused Carolyn to lose weight. She was excited about this loss and decided to increase her "healthy" eating by decreasing her intake of fat. Before too long, Carolyn was eating no fat in her diet. She had developed a feeling that certain foods were "good"—that is, foods that she felt physically and emotionally okay eating—and foods that were "bad." She felt emotionally uncomfortable eating the "bad" foods. This emotional discomfort led to feelings of shame, and eventually bingeing and purging when she ate these foods. What had begun as an innocent diet turned into anorexia nervosa and bulimia.

This emotional hunger is associated with physical and emotional deprivation. Studies have shown that deprivation of certain foods, such as carbohydrates, can result in a decrease in serotonin levels, which may increase binge eating. In addition to this, deprivation of desired foods because they are viewed as "bad" is more likely to prompt binge eating than if those foods were freely eaten and "legalized" (Hirschmann & Munter, 1988). Thus, part of the treatment of hunger is not only to differentiate between the various hungers, but also to help people with eating disorders "legalize" all foods to prevent restriction and/or bingeing.

There are cultural issues related to social hunger. These cultural issues are deeply held and emotionally laden with meaning for immigrant families and peoples of various cultures. In many cultures and families, eating is a way to show respect or appreciation for what is prepared and served, as well as for the preparer/server. When we eat socially we share in the ambiance and mood of communing with friends, families, and colleagues. Food gives us reason to socialize. When responding to cultural hungers, we are using food not only to socialize, but also to convey respect, love, and appreciation. The following story, relayed by co-author of this volume, Mona Villapiano, is an example:

When traveling to Italy with my daughter, her classmates, and several teachers and chaperones, I had the experience, perhaps only to a very small degree, that many clients with eating disorders have. I needed to decide either to eat more than I was comfortable eating in order to please, and not insult another, or eat what was comfortable for me, while knowing it offended the other.

Each evening, we would arrive at a different restaurant, often in a different Italian city, for a five-course meal. The meal was pre-chosen and served by courses, often by the very people who prepared it. The first course was the antipasto, followed by the pasta, then the meat or fish, potatoes, and vegetable; next came the salad, and the final course, the dessert. These meals were always freshly prepared, highlighting the unique ingredients and cooking style of each region, and served with pride and anticipation of our great satisfaction. Truly, these meals were delicious and abundant . . . so abundant, that I learned to eat only a portion of each course so I could sample all courses before I felt uncomfortably full.

In Casino, a small town between Naples and Rome, I followed the eating plan just described, sampling all courses, but finishing none in order to have room to sample everything. As the chef cleared each course, in Italian he would inquire why another chaperone and I had not completed the course. We both assured him that each course was delicious, but since we knew more delicious courses were coming, we wanted to have room to savor each course. He would frown and remove our plates. We felt badly and tried to think of how we could feed ourselves in a way that was comfortable for us without offending him.

By the dessert course, he announced that we, who had not finished every bite of the prior four courses, were to be punished by being served the smallest portions of cake, while others received very large servings. He announced this loudly for the entire group to hear. Although we were happy that he finally served us manageable portions, we felt embarrassed and sad that we had so deeply offended him.

These were my feelings concerning a person toward whom I had no real connection. I think of how I would have felt if it had involved a person toward whom I had a strong personal connection. To be unable to complete all courses prepared by Grandmother and to observe her crestfallen face would have felt even more upsetting than experiencing this with a strange chef.

This left me wondering if this might be how those who suffer from eating disorders feel: that their feelings and needs . . . what is good and right for them . . . must be abandoned or squelched in order to please, or care for, another? How difficult it is to listen to the self in the face of such powerful needs from another. How difficult it is to know that caring for the self is the source of insult or hurt toward the other. Unfortunately, this conflict is played out around food rather than in the social/emotional realm. So, to avoid being "emotionally stuffed" they refuse or expel food.

HUNGER AND THE STAGES OF CHANGE

Precontemplation Stage

If your client is in Precontemplation she needs psychoeducation. She needs to be educated about the differences between physical, emotional, and social/cultural hungers. At this stage, it may also be helpful to provide your client with a list of feelings, for very often feelings have been repressed and/or suppressed, and may need to be learned or re-learned, so she can be helped to identify and differentiate between her experience of these feelings and her desire/avoidance of food. Worksheet #1, provided at the end of the chapter, should be helpful for your client during this stage.

Contemplation Stage

In the Contemplation stage of treatment, it is best to review the first worksheet, and begin to explore with your client what it will be like for her to begin to change. This is a stage of ambivalence, and as such it is important to address not only the "pros" of change, but also the "cons" of change. The eating disorder has helped your client "survive," and as such it is going to be terrifying for the client to begin to think of letting it go. For example, a client of mine has found tremendous relief from overwhelming anxiety once she purges. Nothing has reduced her anxiety as purging has. Asking her to reduce her purging may overwhelm her with anticipated anxiety. Most clients experience intense anxiety as they anticipate change. At this stage of change, the therapist's major task is to help the client explore the cons, or the reasons NOT to change this behavior. What will she face, do, or feel, if she stops feeding emotional hungers with food? What would it be like for your client to sit with emotional hunger, rather than feed herself with food? These are the kinds of questions that get addressed in the stage of Contemplation. Worksheets #2 and #3 can be helpful when working with clients in the stage of contemplation.

Preparation Stage

In the stage of Preparation, the focus is on concrete preparations for change. It is at this stage that the client begins to explore alternatives to her current "survival strategies." It is important to understand that these, more appropriate, alternatives are not going to feel as if they work "as well," and initially, they won't. However, it is still important to help the client identify alternatives to her current coping, which has been so destructive. This may initially take place within your office, as your client may not be able to do this on her own, and often consists of role-plays, hypothetical situations, and cognitively "challenging" your client, to name a few examples. An example of how the therapist works in the stage of preparation is as follows:

You are sitting in session with your client, and focusing on exploring the concept of hunger. You ask your client to take on the role of the "healthy" voice and you take on the role of the "eating disorder's voice." The role-play goes as follows:

Healthy voice: "I know I am not hungry for food."
Eating disorder's voice: "You know you are going to be miserable until you eat."
Healthy voice: "I don't want to eat; I'm not physically hungry."
Eating disorder's voice: "Come on . . . EAT . . . you know that you are going to feel better once you eat."
Healthy voice: "I'm not going to give into you. I know I will feel better if I DON'T eat!"
Eating disorder's voice: "You know you can't concentrate without eating . . . C'mon . . . food will make you feel better . . . "
Healthy voice: "No!"

And on it goes. This role play is a way to begin to challenge the eating-disordered person's way of thinking, while acknowledging how difficult it is going to be to deny feeding one's emotional hunger with food.

Another example that can be used in the stage of Preparation is the acronym H.A.L.T., which is linket to a slogan that 12-Step programs often use: "never get too Hungry, Angry, Lonely, or Tired." H.A.L.T. is used as follows:

H = HUNGER—if/when you feel physically hungry, EAT.
A = ANGER—if/when you feel angry, RELEASE IT. Call a friend, punch a pillow, etc.
L = LONELY—if/when you feel lonely, REACH OUT TO SOMEONE.
T = TIRED—if/when you feel tired, SLEEP.

These four tasks are the cornerstones for living; for those with eating disorders, they are often either overlooked or not learned. Identifying these tasks can be extremely helpful for when the client prepares for the Action stage.

Action Stage

In the stage of Action, clients should PRACTICE, PRACTICE, PRACTICE! Continue using the worksheets at the end of this chapter to encourage your client to practice her work outside of the therapy sessions. In this stage, your client is ready to take the information and knowledge learned in therapy and implement it in everyday life. This is the foundation of recovery.

SUMMARY

A critical focus in working with clients presenting with eating disorders is exploring and differentiating between the three types of hunger: physical, emotional, and social. Without this exploration, behavioral issues with food are unlikely to be resolved. How the therapist approaches the "hungers" will likely influence recovery. Prochaska's stages of change can greatly help therapists address hunger based on the clients' readiness for change. As stated in this chapter, the stage of precontemplation involved education on the hungers; contemplation focuses on helping the client explore what prevents her from changing. In other words, it helps the client explore her fears associated with letting go of the behaviors. Preparation involves strategizing the plan for change, and action is the stage where the plan for change is practiced. Meeting clients at their stages of readiness for exploring hunger, and following the recommendations above, will foster recovery from hunger issues that influence eating disorders.

Worksheet #1 Identifying Feelings

Directions: Circle feelings that you believe encourage you to eat even when you are not physically hungry. Star feelings that you believe would help you resist emotional eating.

Anger	Apathy	Anxiety	Affection
Anguish	Apprehension	Arousal	Amusement
Bitterness	Calm	Compassion	Caring
Contentment	Cheerfulness	Contempt	Cruelty
Disgust	Destructiveness	Despair	Desire
Envy	Enthusiasm	Embarrassment	Excitement
Fear	Frustration	Fury	Fondness
Grief	Gloom	Guilt	Gratitude
Horror	Hate	Helplessness	Hopefulness
Happiness	Hysteria	Humiliation	Hostility
Invalidation	Irritation	Infatuation	Insecurity
Isolation	Joy	Jealousy	Kindness
Loneliness	Longing	Love	Lust
Melancholy	Misery	Mean-spiritedness	Miserliness
Nervousness	Neglect	Outrage	Overwhelmed
Ostracized	Optimism	Pessimism	Passion
Pride	Pity	Panic	Patience
Rage	Righteousness	Remorse	Regret
Resentment	Relief	Rejection	Shyness
Sorrow	Spite	Satisfaction	Sympathy
Tenderness	Tension	Terror	Uneasiness
Unhappiness	Vengefulness	Violent	Worry

Worksheet #2:
The Pros and Cons of Satisfying Physical but not Emotional Hunger with Food

<u>Pros</u>	<u>Cons</u>
I'll feel more in control if I eat when I'm physically hungry.	*I am afraid I won't be able to tolerate the anxiety if I don't eat when I'm anxious.*

1. _____

   _____

2. _____

   _____

3. _____

   _____

4. _____

   _____

5. _____

   _____

6. _____

   _____

7. _____

   _____

1. _____

   _____

2. _____

   _____

3. _____

   _____

4. _____

   _____

5. _____

   _____

6. _____

   _____

7. _____

   _____

Worksheet #3: Belief Systems

This worksheet is to help you recognize your current belief systems and identify ways to counter faulty or inappropriate beliefs.

> *Example:* *Current belief: If I don't binge at night, I won't be able to sleep.*
> *Counterbelief: I understand I may be anxious that I won't sleep if I don't eat at night and I may need to consider other alternatives to help me sleep, but the eating at night really isn't helping me.*

1. Current belief:

   _____

   _____

   Counterbelief:

   _____

   _____

2. Current belief:

   _____

   _____

   Counterbelief:

   _____

   _____

3. Current belief:

   _____

   _____

   Counterbelief:

   _____

   _____

4. Current belief:

   _____

   _____

   Counterbelief:

   _____

   _____

5. Current belief:

   _____

   _____

   Counterbelief:

   _____

   _____

Food: Fear and Restriction

Goals

1. To help therapists understand what issues usually pre-date food fears and restrictions.
2. To learn ways to help clients learn to eat more comfortably, fully, and flexibly by addressing their underlying fears and painful feelings in more adaptive ways.

HISTORY OF FOOD FEARS AND RESTRICTIONS

Clients fear food and restrict their intake for multiple reasons. The reasons they advance may be simple or complex. Often they are unknown. Your goal with your client will be to explore what may have led to her coping through fear and restriction and what might set her free to nourish herself fully and comfortably. The following are some of the reasons advanced for food fears and restrictions. In no way are we attempting to provide an exhaustive list, but we are attempting to discuss the myriad social, cultural, familial, biological, and psychological issues, alone or together, advanced for the genesis of food fears and restriction.

Social Issues

Our society worships thinness, especially in women. It relentlessly targets women with the message that thinness equals health and beauty. Most of the magazines written for women focus on: fashion; diets; exercise; body size and shape; and how to attract, win, and keep a man in one's life. The underlying message in all of these content areas is "thin is in." The same message pervades the airways. Most women portrayed on TV are thin and fit. In movies and videos, thin and fit women are the heroines and villains. Models, actresses, and female icons are generally thin, and sometimes extremely thin. Most represent a female body type unachievable for the majority of women.

Add to this the message of the health, fitness, and the dieting industries' messages, and women are further inundated with the reasons and the means by which they can attain the thin and fit body they so desire. Television, newspaper, radio, magazine, and Internet advertisements tout all kinds of pills, drinks, concoctions, packaged diet foods, machines, equipment, regimens, and memberships developed and made available to help women achieve their desired weight, body size, and shape.

Finally, the medical profession has issued alarming messages about the abysmal shape of the American public. Every year more and more people are termed obese, out-of-shape, sedentary, and afflicted with serious health problems such as heart disease, cancer, and diabetes. Each of these illnesses may be, in part, attributable to high weight and lack of exercise. Therefore, the medical profession has cautioned Americans and those of other western capitalistic countries to reduce their intake of fat and to increase their level of fitness and health through the adoption of healthier eating and exercise regimens.

Women who develop eating disorders appear to take society's mandates quite seriously. Not only will they seek the highly desired thin and fit body ideal, but they will do so with a vengeance. Not only will they decrease their consumption of fat and increase their exercise, but also they will eschew all fat grams and exercise to exhaustion and injury. Not only will they attain thinness, they will attain Twiggy and Kate Moss levels of thinness. Their perfectionism drives them to extremes.

All along they hope their quest will bring them the love, adoration, attention, and respect afforded to the models, actresses, and female icons that grace revered covers and screens. Sadly, this seldom happens . . . and if it does . . . it is short-lived and painful.

Cultural Issues

Culture and society intersect. Teasing out the impact of one separate from the other may be impossible, but identifying where culture is preeminent may be possible.

Those of us who were born in the United States were raised with the belief that anything is possible. Poor men have grown up to become our presidents. Great actors and actresses, businessmen, inventors, artists, and writers have struggled out of low-paying jobs and impoverished life circumstances to wealth and acclaim. People of color and immigrants, despite tremendous struggle and prejudice, have achieved success and power in the United States.

The rewards of power and success are abundance: plenty of food, material goods, recognition, and adoration. Our culture rewards with excess.

As Americans became successful, they could reward their families with abundant food. If food was on the table, it not only represented success but love. To provide for one's family is the way in which many Americans show love for their children. Many immigrants, also, display their love for their children and for their original and adopted homelands by continuing the culinary traditions of their native lands in America, the land of plenty.

We, as a blended nation, become one in our celebrations with food. Thanksgiving, the holiday that celebrates the birth of our nation, is a feast day. The most bountiful tables and heaping plates show our success as a nation . . . a people . . . and a family. But it is these excesses which fly in the face of our new national pastime: thinness and fitness at any cost.

We are now a nation of conflicting messages: eat hearty, relax, and celebrate our abundance . . . but do not be slothful and glutinous. Deny gustatory pleasures . . . live on as little as possible . . . run and work off the excess . . . become sleek and androgynous in form. Thus, we have adopted as our new moral code: Have, but do not indulge; work-off all that is not absolutely necessary for life. Those who have plenty but look gaunt and spare are the most revered.

Those with eating disorders recognize the moral order and abide by it.

The Family

The family is a microcosm of the culture. Many American families have plenty of food. Some have too much. Sadly, some do not have enough. Providing or withholding food, and the atmosphere in which food is provided or withheld, may give us clues into the workings of the family, and some idea of the epigenesis of the eating disorder.

For example, in the family where a parent *provides* a $10.00 bill for the child to order a pizza or walk to a fast food restaurant for a burger and shake for dinner, such an act may tell us that food is *replacing* that which is in short order: *time, attention, caring,* or *connection* with the parents. There may be plenty of food, or plenty of money to buy the food, but the social and emotional connection to parents afforded children who share dinner with their family is absent. Food becomes a *filler* . . . a *comfort for the void*. Food, or the provision of food, replaces the other forms of nurturance children and families need . . . connection . . . communication . . . and time.

Many children share meals with their parents, but the mood at the meal is oppressive, full of conflict, or cold. In these families, it looks O.K. but it isn't. There is plenty of food and the parents are there, but the social and emotional nurturance—the connection—is not there. This taints the food. Food becomes *associated with loneliness, fear, emptiness, or anger*. In these cases food *represents painful emotions*.

In families with a parent who is depressed, a substance abuser, or medically ill, children observe the ways in which their parent uses or avoids food. For some children, a depressed parent never eats or eats continuously. A child with a substance-abusing parent may see no eating or chaotic eating. The child with an ill parent may see a parent unable to eat or in pain every time he or she does eat. Either these children mimic their parents or try to do the exact opposite of the parent. In either case, usually the child develops a pattern of extremes and, in these cases, *their extremes with food represent the extreme situations* in their homes.

Many contemporary families are now headed by parents, particularly mothers, who themselves do not eat, eat chaotically, eat clandestinely, binge eat, purge what they've eaten, or use a combination of these tactics. Children, especially daughters, often grow up mirroring their mother's eating behavior. Many don't recognize it as disordered. *Their use of food represents connection or identification with the parent or learned behavior.*

Children in families where criticism and ridicule are afforded their mothers or themselves for eating or gaining weight, often deny themselves food to protect themselves from ridicule or criticism. *In these families food and eating represents shame, embarrassment, criticism, and ridicule.*

In other families, there are control battles waged over food. Mother or father decides what goes on the child's plate and in what amounts. Children are punished for eating too much or too little. Sweets or treats are not allowed or strictly limited. The family meal becomes a battleground . . . a test of wills. . . . This sets the stage for the incredible control many with eating disorders have over food . . . where not one morsel passes their lips unless it is inspected, rejected or accepted within very strict guidelines. *In these cases, food provides the child a sense of her own agency or control.*

In still other families, food or the ingestion of other substances, is the method of abuse. For example, one child was repeatedly raped after being forced to ingest tranquilizers and vodka. She would often vomit during or after the rape (which was sometimes oral). Following the event, she would be given a glass of milk and cookies to "make it all better." Soon everything that went into her mouth felt like "poison" and she could not eat or drink. *In these cases food evokes abuse.*

Other examples of abuse linked to the properties of food include girls who understand that being adequately nourished gives them curves (seen as appealing to abusers) and their menses (seen as making them fertile and thus capable of pregnancy). These girls stop eating to reduce their curves and bring on amenorrhea to protect against being impregnated by the abuser. *In these cases, denial of food is protection.*

A woman who fears and restricts food may be telling you something about her family circumstances or her environment.

Psychological Issues

When women do not feed themselves, they may, at first, believe that it is because they are fat. The word "fat" has deeper meaning for those who develop eating disorders. "Fat" may mean, "I am burdened or overwhelmed with the feelings, needs, or wishes of another." It may mean, "I am unworthy, unwanted, a burden to my family, society, or the world." It may mean, "I am hateful, disgusting, or worthless because I believe, or was told, I am bad, dirty, a slut, or a whore." It may mean, "I am imperfect, flawed, unforgiving, intolerant, or unkind because I feel anger, resentment, hatred, rage, or lack of love toward someone who neglected, ignored, hurt, abused, shamed, degraded, or terrified me." It may mean, "I have lost a friend, parent, lover, husband, baby, a breast, health, security, and, therefore, I wish to die, disappear, become invisible, numb, or unconscious to escape this pain or loss."

The emotions, beliefs, or life situations underpinning the words, "I feel fat," are experienced as *heavy, weighty,* and *crushing.* If we collaborate in our work with our client, we will understand why she "feels fat."

Once we understand why she feels the way she feels, we must also help her to accept her feelings. We have heard many clients with eating disorders berate themselves for having an eating disorder because, " . . . I have a great life, great parents, family, husband, job, home," and on and on. They believe that because they were born into a good home, or privilege, or love, that they should not hurt, cry, mourn, grieve, rage, or despair. We tell them that whatever caused them to "feel fat" must have been a *heavy, weighty, crushing feeling* for them, even if no one else felt it to be so. Owning feelings . . . and feeling feelings . . . is a weighty *burden* to bear for those who fear and restrict food. They wish to feel spare and empty, for feelings "fill" them with painful, unwanted, unacceptable emotions.

Biological Issues

Those of us who are parents of more than one child know that children are born with different temperaments. We may have one child who expresses herself freely and deeply, refuses to shoulder the burdens and expectations of others, and considers herself as well as others. We may have another who, although perhaps eloquent, says nothing about what she truly feels, willingly carries the burdens and expectations of the world, and considers others before herself.

The "good little girl," the "excellent student," the "perfect child" who "caused no trouble" is more often than not the child who, if she were to develop an eating disorder, would develop one typified by fear of food and restriction because, she *carries, holds* and *shoulders* too much and she must shed the weight of food and body in hopes it will *lighten her emotional load.*

We do not know if some children are born with a biological predisposition that puts them at risk for the development of an eating disorder. We do know, however, that many girls who develop restricting types of eating disorders seem to be perfectionistic, rigidly controlled, and exquisitely sensitive to the needs of others' while often oblivious to their own needs.

We also know that children who grow up in families where another biological relative has an eating disorder or depression may be more at risk for the development of those illnesses herself.

The biological piece that we do know is that all organisms that are starved develop social, emotional, and cognitive changes due to the starvation. We know that starved girls become more disordered in their thinking about their bodies and more frightened of food. We know that starved girls think constantly about food and attempt to satisfy their cravings for food and nurturance by feeding and nurturing others. We know that starved girls exhibit more signs of depression and irritability, and frequently become isolative and uncommunicative. Finally, we know that the starvation, unless corrected, will keep these girls from progressing to health no matter how well understood are the social, cultural, psychological, and familial pieces to the puzzle. Therefore, in order to progress in our work with these clients, we must focus first on how to help them adequately nourish themselves. There are many ways to do this. The frontal assault of taking control and forcing food seldom works; however, in some cases we must take over and feed them until they can feed themselves. This means hospitalization, psychiatric or medical, for its lifesaving potential.

The Gestalt

In summary, we believe that one factor alone, whether social, cultural, familial, psychological, or biological, does not cause an eating disorder. Instead, we believe that it may be a confluence of factors that sets the stage for its development. Addressing and understanding all the potential contributing factors will help the client progress toward recovery.

A PLAN FOR CHANGE

Reducing fear of food and decreasing restrictive eating are the goals to work on with clients with restrictive types of eating disorders.

Precontemplation Stage

For the client who presents in Precontemplation, education about the dangers of food restriction and the inconvenience, discomfort, isolation, and loneliness of food fears is the way to start. This client either does not want to be in your office, is unready to change, or honestly does not see a problem with restrictive eating. The reasons to change must be offered but in a non-lecturing, caring, and factual way. For example, I will ask clients, or have them write whether they've ever experienced certain thoughts or feelings or behaved in certain ways when they were dieting. After that I will let them read or I will describe for them how physically and psychologically normal, healthy men who agreed to be in a semistarvation experiment (Keys, Brozek, Henschel, Mickelsen, & Taylor, 1950) felt, thought, and behaved. It is often astonishing for the client to see that these men felt, thought, and behaved like they did under conditions of semistarvation. (You and your client can read about this study in our companion client workbook, *Eating Disorders: The Journey to Recovery Workbook*.) They learn how semistarvation and restriction are the same thing and the source of many of the problems they say they would like to overcome (e.g., depression, preoccupation with food). For clients in Precontemplation, Worksheet #1 may be very helpful.

Contemplation Stage

Clients who present in Contemplation are ambivalent about change. They need help, not only looking at the "pros" of change but the "cons" of change. They may be beginning to feel scared or anxious about eating more, even though they see the reasons to do so. It is at this time that they need to discuss with you the issues from the social, cultural, familial, and psychological history-taking that you have done. A thorough exploration of these issues will uncover the reasons why the client *should not* give up restrictive eating. These are the "cons" of change. For example, the girl who believes her father left her mother because the mother was "too fat," will be fearful if she stops restrictively eating; she too will be "too fat" and be abandoned by her father. The adolescent who feels she cannot compete at her sport if she is "too fat" will be fearful that eating more will cause her to fail at her sport. The woman who feels overwhelmed with pain and rage about her childhood of abuse every time she has food in her stomach, will fear that without her empty stomach and the numbness that if brings, she will not be able to survive the feelings. Once clients talk about what they will have to feel, face, and do without restrictive eating, they will be able to move onto developing strategies to tolerate the painful, difficult emotions and the expectations that they believe will come true if they give up restrictive eating. The Worksheet #2 writing exercise will be helpful to clients in Contemplation.

Preparation Stage

Clients in Preparation are aware of the pros and cons of change and are perched for battle. However, they need their war plans to succeed. At this point developing lists of strategies clients can use to cope with awakening feelings and expectations is critical. Help your clients work on developing lists of cognitive (thinking), behavioral (doing), and support (people) strategies to assist them in their plans for action. Suggest Worksheet #3 as an aid to clients preparing for the battle with their eating disorder.

Action Stage

At this stage, clients are *doing*. They are increasing their eating, trying feared foods, and feeling uncomfortable and scared. They need much encouragement and support at this time. They may also need you to help them pace their actions so they do not become overwhelmed. They need many safe and supportive opportunities to practice this behavior. Worksheet #4 will help them to keep track of their feelings and thoughts as they eat, as well as the strategies and supports that work for them versus the ones that do not help. In summary, the Action stage requires practicing the desired behaviors.

Maintenance Stage

At this stage, clients are engaged in doing, which becomes easier over time. They have found a schedule, structure, and supports that bolster their ability to continue eating. They may also have found the triggers that set them up for a relapse and thus, they are preparing for how to deal with them more effectively. At this stage, clients do well writing their thoughts, feelings, and activities in a diary or journal. This helps to keep them focused and reflective of their experience

SUMMARY

As stated earlier, there are many factors associated with eating disorders. These include: social, cultural, familial, psychological, and biological. Exploration of the impact each factor has on the client presenting with an eating disorder is an essential task for the therapist in helping the client achieve recovery. This chapter has focused on the specific symptoms of restriction. Restriction can be defined as refusal to nourish the body adequately, or (for others) it can mean having a limited variety of foods which results in an unbalanced intake. It is imperative that therapy specifically address the symptom of restriction for those presenting with anorexia nervosa and/or bulimia. This chapter has taken the therapist through the journey to recovery for clients, based on the clients' stage of readiness for change. A brief recap is as follows: precontemplation, education about the dangers of restricting; contemplation, exploring why *not* to give up restrictive behaviors; preparation, strategizing the means to increasing intake and/or decreasing restrictions; and action, initiating change through challenging cognitions and behaviors that lead to restriction. Although never the issue, restriction greatly hinders recovery; it is difficult to work with clients who starve their brain! As such, the goal of increasing the clients intake will positively address other aspects of recovery as well.

Worksheet # 1
Feelings and Behaviors Questionnaire

Please indicate, with a "yes" or a "no" whether you have experienced the following feelings and/or behaviors when attempting to diet or eat restrictively:

1. Depression
2. Elation
3. Irritability
4. Frequent outbursts or anger
5. Increase in anxiety
6. Nail biting
7. Smoking (either you start to smoke or you increase your number of cigarettes per day)
8. Apathy (loss of interest in things once enjoyed)
9. Hypochondriasis (fear of developing illnesses, intense focus on bodily changes and extreme concern over their meaning)
10. Hysteria (becoming overwhelmed or overwrought with the slightest provocation and expressing it intensely by screeching, exclaiming, running out of the room, etc.)
11. Shoplifting or stealing, even things that you do not need or want
12. Bizarre or unusual thoughts
13. Increased isolation (physical and emotional withdrawal from others)
14. Decreased sexual interest
15. Difficulty concentrating
16. Poor judgement
17. Increased preoccupation with food
18. Hoarding of food
19. Increased consumption of coffee, tea, or diet soda
20. Increased gum chewing

Now that you have completed your self-rating, read about the Keys et al. (1950) study in our companion client workbook, *Eating Disorders: The Journey to Recovery Workbook.*

Worksheet #2
What If I Change?

Directions: Write about what you believe you will have to face, do, and feel if you no longer eat restrictively. What will others expect of you? What will you expect of yourself? What feelings might emerge? What will happen if you feel these feelings?

_____

_____

_____

_____

_____

_____

_____

_____

_____

_____

_____

_____

_____

_____

_____

_____

_____

_____

_____

_____

_____

_____

_____

_____

_____

_____

_____

_____

_____

_____

_____

Worksheet #3
Strategies, Structures and Supports

Directions: Write a thorough list of cognitive (thinking) and behavioral (doing) strategies you can use to resist eating restrictively. Do not edit your list. Write down any thoughts that come to mind. You can shorten your list as you and your therapist determine which ones will be most practical and effective.

Cognitive (Thinking) Strategies: (Examples: Think *"If I eat restrictively, I will 'restrict' my ability to love, learn, work, and live well. Eating restrictively is continuing the abuse."*)

1. _____
2. _____
3. _____
4. _____
5. _____
6. _____
7. _____
8. _____
9. _____
10. _____

Behavioral (Doing) Strategies: (Examples: *1. Eat meals with "safe" people who will support my efforts but not attempt to coerce or control me. 2. Do not read labels on packaged food items. 3. Remove wrappers immediately and store foods in storage bags or containers.*)

1. _____
2. _____
3. _____
4. _____
5. _____
6. _____
7. _____
8. _____
9. _____
10. _____

Next, write a list of all the people in your life who can support your efforts at recovery. Each of these people may not be right for each type of support you need, so list the people beside the type of support they can offer. For example, your sister might be a wonderful, non-judgmental listener, but because she lives so far away she might not be able to share meals with you. Your friend and coworker eats normally and comfortably, so she would be a good person to practice eating with but she would never understand your feelings, so you'll save them for your sister. Your mother cannot emotionally support you, but she is willing to pay for your therapy because you cannot afford it and she can.

Supportive People in my Life and What I can Ask of Them:

1. _____

2. _____

3. _____

4. _____

5. _____

6. _____

7. _____

8. _____

9. _____

10. _____

Worksheet #4
My Daily Plan for Action—Examples

Directions: Record each meal and snack. For each meal and snack of each day, write what you were feeling before you ate, while you were eating, and after you ate. Write which strategies helped and which did not.

Here is an example:

Breakfast (list foods): plain bagel and cream cheese, orange juice, tea

Feelings (indicate before, during, and after eating): Before eating I felt anxious. While I was eating I felt over-whelmed and I thought that I couldn't do it. Once I finished I felt bloated and fat.

Strategies (list and indicate ones that helped and ones that didn't): It helped me to tell myself that "Food is my medicine." It also helped that I had agreed to eat with Lorna, my coworker. She made eating feel normal and fun because she's such a good conversationalist and she doesn't focus on my food. It doesn't help to eat in silence.

Now, you try. Copy these worksheets so you can do one each day.

Worksheet #4
My Daily Plan for Action

Breakfast: _____

      Feelings: _____

_____

_____

      Strategies: _____

_____

_____

Snack: _____

      Feelings: _____

_____

_____

      Strategies: _____

_____

_____

Lunch: _____

      Feelings: _____

_____

_____

      Strategies: _____

_____

_____

Snack: _____

      Feelings: _____

_____

_____

      Strategies: _____

_____

_____

Dinner: _____

      Feelings: _____

_____

_____

      Strategies: _____

_____

_____

Snack: _____

      Feelings: _____

_____

_____

      Strategies: _____

_____

_____

Binge Eating and Purging

Goals

1. To help clients understand the effects of binge eating and purging.
2. To help clients assess their readiness to change binge eating and purging behaviors.
3. To help clients develop a plan to address binge eating and purging that meets them at their stage of change.

Clients who binge eat and purge are generally ashamed of their behavior. They do not reveal these behaviors easily for fear of judgement, criticism, or abandonment. Because of these fears, clients with eating disorders don't always know how much binge eating and purging they are engaging in. To not know protects them from shame.

When clients acknowledge to you their binge eating and purging behaviors, carefully and completely assess *how often, where,* and *when* they binge and purge. What they eat in a binge is also important, but the other questions are more critical during the initial assessment.

CASE ILLUSTRATIONS

Case 1: Bonnie

A young woman named Bonnie came to me (M. Villapiano) for treatment of her eating disorder. She had been hospitalized twice before, once for depression and a suicide attempt and the second time for the eating disorder. She was clearly depressed and feeling hopeless about ever recovering from her eating disorder, which had taken over her life.

As we talked in the initial session, I learned that Bonnie would binge late at night and then drive to the back of a darkened, inner-city parking lot to vomit. She lived with her mother and did not dare to vomit at home, fearful that her mother might learn she had not "recovered" from her eating disorder during her last hospitalization. We talked about the risks of vomiting, but I conveyed to her that I was even more worried about her safety in a darkened inner-city parking lot.

Bonnie seemed surprised at my concern. She was not used to taking her safety seriously. At the end of this session she agreed that if she needed to vomit late at night she would do so in the safety of her own home, despite her worries about her mother. She also agreed to allow her mother to be involved in her treatment and planned on asking her mother to come to the session with her.

Had I just asked about frequency of vomiting and amounts eaten, I would have missed this far more critical information about my new client. Bonnie and I realized, by the end of the first session, that focusing on her safety, in general, would have to be our top priority in therapy, even if it meant we could not focus on decreasing the eating-disordered behaviors at this time.

As we explored where and when she binged and purged, Bonnie also reported that she would frequently binge eat in her car. Again, she felt this was a way to keep her behaviors secret from her mother. She reported how she would drive from fast-food restaurant to fast-food restaurant to stock up on cheeseburgers, French fries, milk shakes, apple pies, and burritos. She would then head for the 4-lane, super highway which ringed the city, and drive at excessive speeds. She told me that food was like a narcotic. It helped her feel better by occluding her sorrow, anxiety, shame, and terror. It also blinded her to potential dangers. I learned that she had had 4 minor to major automobile accidents in the past 18 months. Twice the police had requested that she submit to a Breathalyzer, which indicated that she was not intoxicated. She told me what the police did not know. When she was binge eating and driving, she was unaware of her surroundings and her actions. She stated, "I think I'm more dangerous on the roads binge eating than I would be if I were drinking." I told her we did not need to test out this assumption to know that she should not be binge eating and driving at the same time.

Is this young woman suicidal? Whether she was intending to die or not, she was putting herself and others at risk. She denied any suicidal intent. She convincingly stated that she did not wish to die, only to forget. She did not know how to "forget" without stuffing down and forcefully expelling her feelings with the food and vomiting. Food, in this case, like alcohol and drugs, facilitated the stuffing down or drowning of feelings. Vomiting forcefully expelled them.

Where was Bonnie on the stages of change? She was in Precontemplation concerning her desire to give up her eating disorder, but she was painfully aware of the dangers associated with where and when she exhibited her eating disordered behaviors. Although she hadn't connected her choices of where and when to binge eat and purge with additional dangers, she became aware through our meetings. Because she did not feel ready to stop her binge eating and purging, she learned that she could be unready for ending these behaviors but ready to protect herself and others from her choices about where and when to engage in bingeing and purging.

So, we began to work in the stage of Contemplation concerning using her car in the service of her eating disorder. She was ready to look at the pros and cons of binge eating and/or purging in her car (such as traveling to the darkened parking lot at night). She was becoming more aware of the dangers associated with the use of her car. These were the reasons she would consider not using her car in the service of bingeing and purging. She also recognized that the use of her car protected her from her mother's reactions. She considered this a reason to continue binge eating and purging in her car. The following is her pros and cons list concerning using her car to binge eat and purge.

<u>Using my car to binge eat and purge</u>

Pros	Cons

Mother won't know I still have an eating disorder.
Mother won't be disappointed that I failed to
    recover in the hospital.
	I am not safe.
	I am risking
	    the safety of others.

It looks as if Bonnie could go either way. So, we looked at whether there might be other ways to deal with her mother's feelings while protecting her's and the public's safety.

What I learned was that Bonnie did not believe her mother could bear any more grief. Her father had died recently and her mother was bereft and depressed. Bonnie thought that if her mother didn't know about her eating disorder, she could spare her mother additional grief. As we looked a bit closer, we realized that Bonnie was, in fact, tempting the gods by putting herself at risk for death in a car accident or an assault in a darkened parking lot. Her father had died in a drunken driving accident.

Bonnie was ambivalent about changing her behavior, but she soon announced that she wanted to prepare to change. We entered the stage of Preparation where she and I worked on strategies and skills to help her resist the urge to binge eat and vomit with the use of her car. Here are Bonnie's plans for change:

1. Invite mother to therapy session. Help her learn that recovery comes in stages and teach her what stage of change I am in.
2. Determine how to resist urges to use car to binge eat and vomit.
   a. Have dinner at night. "If I am starving I will have a harder time resisting the urges to binge."
   b. If I still choose to eat late at night I will attempt to eat a non-guilt-inducing snack (yogurt and fruit, cereal and milk, etc.).
   c. Whether or not I am able to eat a non-guilt-inducing snack, I will attempt to resist the urge to purge by engaging in the following activities: go online, see if I can instant message my friends; go online and write e-mails to friends about how I am feeling; write feelings in journal; paint (have paints and easel set up in room at all times); listen to music; pray.
3. If, despite my efforts, I choose to purge, I will resist the urge to use my car by,
   a. Reminding myself that if I must occlude or expel my feelings, I can do so in safer ways. I may write or paint all my unbearable feelings and rip them up or destroy them. I may cry. If none of this helps me, I may vomit in the bathroom in my home.
   b. Practice "distress tolerance" skills that I am learning from the Linehan workbook. (Linehan, 1993a). Remember feelings are like waves. No matter how overwhelming and scary they are, they eventually dissipate.

In time, Bonnie was ready to try these new behaviors. Once she was in the Action stage, she felt more determined to find other ways to express her feelings. Although she did not feel ready to change her eating-disordered behaviors, because she was willing to work on her safety, her eating-disordered behaviors naturally diminished.

Case 2: Ingrid

Ingrid was referred to me by a local hospital for outpatient treatment for her bulimia nervosa. Ingrid was 16, not at all motivated to work on this behavior, and convinced that her bulimia would not hurt her.

Ingrid was clearly in the stage of Precontemplation. She was coming to therapy because she had to. Like many minors, therapy is an imposition, not a choice. Ingrid had been hospitalized for complications related to her eating disorder. She had experienced esophageal tears and bleeding because of her vomiting. She had had an electrolyte imbalance that required hospitalization because she either refused to take her potassium tablets or she vomited them up. Ingrid was a very angry young woman. She talked about her anger at her parents who left her to her own devices. Both were professors who were very invested in their research and teaching. The youngest of 3 children, Ingrid was alone most of the time. Her brother and sister were away at college, her parents' careers kept them away most of the time, and she had no close friends or extended family in the area. Although Ingrid claimed to be glad her parents gave her so much freedom, she seemed angry.

As we talked about her goals for therapy, she made it clear that she had none. She was not ready to work on her eating disorder. She denied that it was a problem and felt her doctors had overreacted. Her parents were "clueless" according to Ingrid and would not even have known she'd had an eating disorder if her doctor hadn't informed them against her will. The only thing Ingrid said she wanted to work on was getting people to leave her alone.

I asked her how I might help her do that and she said she didn't know. I told her it was possible her parents and doctors might leave her alone if her eating disorder symptoms were not so serious. She agreed and therefore said she would work at keeping her potassium pills down. That meant she would need to either vomit at times other than after she took the potassium supplements, or she would decrease her vomiting so she would not need the potassium supplements. She thought about these options and agreed to try to decrease her vomiting.

When I asked her where and when she vomited, she told me that mostly she vomited in her parents' shower. I found this rather interesting and wondered with her why this was her preferred vomiting place. She stated she really didn't know, but thought it was because it was upstairs. She did not have her own bathroom upstairs and this is where she spent most of her time, in her bedroom. Her routine was to come home after school, grab large amounts of junk food . . . chips, cookies, ice cream, soda . . . take them to her room and eat while watching TV. Then she would go to her parents' bathroom to vomit. Why did she choose the shower over the toilet? She said in the shower she could wash off her hands and face while she was vomiting and that felt better to her.

I asked how her parents hadn't found out that she vomited there? She said, "They're clueless . . . and I clean up after myself really well." She said she found it enjoyable to have her parents ranting and raving about why their shower was always so clogged. They'd had a plumber in four times over the past year. She said even now they don't get it.

I said I wondered how she'd ever get her parents to notice how much she hurt and how much anger she felt toward them if she didn't vomit so much and have medical problems. She said, "Well, I'll vomit less, but I'll still do it in their shower."

Without even doing a pros and cons list about continuing to vomit, it became evident to me why Ingrid was not ready to give up her vomiting. It was how she secretly expressed rage and how she hoped her parents would notice her pain without telling them.

I told her I could help her develop strategies to protect her esophagus and her electrolyte balance, but I was also hearing that she needed her parents to notice and pay attention to her pain and anger. By reducing her vomiting we could help with the first problem but not the second. She was intrigued. This led to her willingness to write a pros and cons list about why to and why not to reduce her vomiting. Here is her list.

Why to, and not to, reduce my vomiting

Reduce (pros)	Not Reduce (cons)
Protect my esophagus. Protect my electrolyte balance.	Bleed so parents will notice. Electrolytes out of balance so parents will notice.

Why Reduce Vomiting but still do it in shower

Reduce but do in shower (pros)	Reduce but don't do in shower (cons)
Esophagus will have chance to heal. Leave vomit in shower. Parents will notice.	Esophagus will have chance to heal. Parents won't notice.

Ingrid was excited by the prospect of her parents coming home to find vomit in their shower. She could see the disbelief on her mother's face. She could hear her father bellow in anger. She was delighted. She was also terrified. Would they banish her in disgust? She was not at all sure of their love or commitment to her. She knew that she was an impediment to their lifestyle. She was definitely the "third wheel."

The prospect of making known her pain and anger in the form of their finding vomit in the shower was not as delightful as she explored her deeper fears.

This process compelled the 16-year-old girl with the *belle indifference* about her eating disorder to cry about her fear that she was unwanted and unloved. The pain and anger that these acknowledgements raised were symbolically transmitted by her "vomit in the shower." Might there be a better way? Might there be a way to express these fears and feelings that would not cause her banishment?

This was the next issue that she contemplated. Ingrid spent much time in the stage of Contemplation. How important were all these contemplations to her eventual recovery? How important was it that she was not being rushed to decrease her vomiting without knowing how important it was for her to express and convey her message? Like many unwilling or precontemplative adolescents, Ingrid had to feel she was ready to, wanted to, and knew how to decrease her eating-disordered behaviors without giving up her message.

Eventually, Ingrid prepared her plan to reduce these behaviors while increasing the chances that her parents would notice, but not banish her. Her parents were willing to participate in family therapy where they eventually learned of their daughter's deep-seated fears that she was neither wanted nor loved. Her parents stated they had never known that she'd felt this way. Their willingness to change their behaviors to notice more, be there more, and show more care helped Ingrid prepare to change.

Two years later, Ingrid is away at college and no longer vomits in showers.

Case 3: *Adrienne*

Adrienne arrived in therapy ready for Action. A 32-year-old, single, real estate broker, Adrienne had decided to stop living with bulimia. She was determined to stop her bingeing and purging behavior and had made excellent progress stopping during the day, but seemed unable to stop at night.

Adrienne had been bingeing and purging since her sophomore year in college following a year of strenuous exercise and restrictive eating to retain her position on the cheerleading squad. She fell from a pyramid and fractured her pelvis. Depressed, she was sidelined in a cast for 6 months. With no one aware of her depression, and finding food the only solace, she began to binge eat on a regular basis. Once she had the cast removed, Adrienne realized that she had gained 15 pounds. Terrified, she began to purge by vomiting after a friend said she'd tried it for a short time after she'd gained weight following an incapacitating injury.

Adrienne intended to try vomiting only for a short time. She found, however, that she could not stop even after she lost the 15 pounds and more. Thirteen years later, she was still vomiting. Her desire to lose weight had eventually backfired and no matter how much she vomited, she could not compensate for the enormous amounts of food she ate during a binge. Distraught and discouraged, but undaunted, Adrienne decided to change her life. She planned how she could avoid binge eating by limiting the food supply in her house, buying food only in individual serving sizes and shopping daily for the day's food. She also took to carrying only the amount of cash that she needed and she cut up her credit and ATM cards. She let her closest friends know what she was trying to do and elicited their help in joining her for meals and doing activities with her to decrease her isolation and introduce more fun in her life. She rightfully believed that if she enjoyed herself more, she might binge less.

Following 9 months of normalized eating during the day with no vomiting, Adrienne sought out my therapeutic help to extend her change to the evenings.

What we learned was that Adrienne felt very lonely when home alone at night. She had no evening activities, most of her friends were married with children and did not have evening time free, and she was so exhausted at the end of most days that she just wanted to sleep. She realized that she was also filled with a diffuse and unsettled feeling at night. She felt anxious and unable to quell her fears about bedtime. In time she understood that heavy bingeing and purging before bed made her so lethargic and exhausted that she could not help but sleep.

This led Adrienne to understand her ambivalence about stopping. Binge eating and purging were her sleeping aids. Why did she have so much difficulty sleeping? Why was she so unsettled at night? She wasn't sure but had vague recollections of fights at night between her parents whose relationship had turned acrimonious and bitter after her father's affair. She recalled wanting to block out the screaming, but she couldn't. As a child she remembers crawling into her older sister's bed, cuddling up and feeling reassured that her sister would take care of her. Two years ago this much loved and protective sister died. Adrienne realized how much she'd relied on evening phone calls to her sister when she was unsettled. She could not call her sister anymore. Nighttime binge eating and purging seemed to offer the comfort, protection, and solace which she seemed unable to find on her own.

We went back to the stage of Contemplation to help Adrienne understand why it would be good to stop her evening binge eating and purging. What had been missing, however, was a thorough assessment of why it could be bad to stop these behaviors. Adrienne needed to find other ways to quell her unsettled and anxious feelings at night so she could sleep. She needed to know she could do this before she could give up her evening binge eating and purging.

Once she understood why she was still bingeing and purging at night, she could clearly see that there were pros and cons to stopping this behavior. Eventually she decided she was ready for Preparation. She worked in therapy to develop plans to strategize how to decrease these nighttime behaviors while learning other skills and finding supportive people in her life who could help her deal with these uncomfortable feelings at night. Her plan looked like this.

<u>Plan to stop binge eating and purging at night</u>

1. Eat dinner with a friend as many nights as possible.
2. Join enjoyable nighttime activities such as a local book club and an acting workshop.
3. Join Alanon, a group for children who have lived in alcoholic families. Her father had abused alcohol and she felt this contributed to his abusive and erratic behavior. In Alanon she hoped to find other adult children who might feel as she did.
4. Attend Alanon meetings any evening when she was without a friend for dinner or another enjoyable activity.
5. Talk with her older brother and find out if he remembers growing up, the fights, and whether he had any trouble sleeping. Try to find affirmation and support.
6. Review affirmations (developed in therapy) each evening to remind self that she deserved to sleep and had the capacity to find other soothing, but not hurtful, activities to help her sleep.
7. Practice 5-senses soothing behaviors each evening (Linehan, 1993a). Identify and use soothing fragrances, textures or touch, music or the voices of soothing friends or even TV shows, and find books, magazines, photographs, pictures, videos or TV shows to look at or watch. Find soothing tastes that don't contribute to bingeing, such as hot herbal teas or peppermint drops.

Once Adrienne was ready she decided to start this plan on a Monday night when she attended her first Alanon meeting. She had also asked her brother and her best friend to be available by phone to talk with her if she needed them. They had agreed and they were very encouraging of her efforts.

Within a year, Adrienne no longer engaged in any bingeing and purging at night. She had developed a close network of friends, had nighttime activities she loved, had reestablished a relationship with her brother, and learned there were other ways to soothe herself and decrease her nighttime anxieties other than by binge eating and purging. During this time she had also agreed to seek the help of a psychiatrist to see if medication for anxiety might help. He had prescribed a nonaddictive anxiolytic. In the beginning it helped her immensely. Now she takes it as needed. She feels she has the tools to make her life better now. She is in the stage of Maintenance. She felt ready to leave therapy and confident that if she ever needed to come back she could. She understood that there was much help and support available to her. She just needed to take advantage of it. It has been 5 years since she terminated therapy. She is married and is expecting her first child. She realizes this welcome but scary change in her life might cause her confidence to slip, but she knows how to bolster herself when she is unsure. She is hopeful, as am I.

If your client is in Precontemplation, review the psychoeducational information about the effects of binge eating and purging. These would include information on the effects of laxatives, diuretics, ipecac, and vomiting on the body. It is most important to explain to clients how purging alters fluid balance but does not decrease weight (i.e., body fat). Explain how dehydration (the lowering of the fluid balance) usually leads to edema (the collection of excess fluid in the body) in those who engage in purging behaviors. Suggest that clients read about this information in the Psychoeducation chapter in our companion workbook, *Eating Disorders: The Journey to Recovery Workbook* (Goodman and Villapiano, 2001).

A precontemplative client can benefit from brief written information and stories written by other people who have had similar eating disorder symptoms. They might be willing to fill out Worksheet #1. If they are unwilling you might ask them to think about the questions.

Clients in the Contemplation, Preparation, and Action stages of recovery might find Worksheets #2, #3, and #4 helpful.

SUMMARY

In this chapter we have reviewed how to apply stages of change theory to our work with clients who binge eat and purge. For clients who were unready or unwilling to acknowledge that the eating disorder was a problem for them, finding a goal that client and therapist could share (even if it was only obliquely related to the eating disorder), seemed to help the client in Precontemplation move to the Contemplation stage. For the clients in the stage of Contemplation, personal vignettes illustrated that each client's readiness to change appeared to be dependent upon feeling she and the therapist understood and affirmed the reasons why she needed her eating disorder. Once this was understood and articulated, the client was able to develop her plans and strategies for change, the Preparation stage. At the Action stage, clients were ready to try on their new behaviors. Having integrated the new, more adaptive behaviors into her repertoire, one client achieved the stage of Maintenance and terminated from formal therapy.

The worksheets at the end of the chapter helped our clients in their stages of change work. Others' worksheets, like those developed by Marsha Linehan in her workbook (1993a), although not specific to eating disorders, are enormously useful to our clients as well.

Worksheet #1
Bingeing and Purging: The What, When and Where

When I binge eat, I usually eat the following foods (circle):

cookies	cakes	candy	ice cream	frozen yogurt	
donuts	muffins	breads	chips	pretzels	nuts
cold cuts	cheeses	pizza	sandwiches	burgers	fried chicken
tacos	pasta	cereal	crackers	granola bars	French fries
eggs	pancakes	waffles	sausage	bacon	peanut butter
entrees	salads	vegetables	fruit	milk	yogurt
juice	soda	alcoholic beverages		other_____	

Here is a range of how much of these foods I would eat during a binge (Example: 3 bowls of cereal, 1 liter of soda, 3 chocolate bars, medium bag of taco chips and salsa):

_____

_____

_____

This is my preferred method of purging_____

My usual binge/purge routine is as follows (Example: I binge on the foods I listed above and then I vomit by sticking my finger down my throat. I vomit 2 or 3 times to make sure I get all the food up. Then I go to sleep or I get shaky and scared.):

_____

_____

_____

_____

I binge and purge_____times per (circle): day, week, month, other_____.

I think I binge because_____.

I think I purge because_____.

Worksheet #2
I Want/Need . . . I Don't Want/Need My Eating Disorder

I want/need my eating
disorder because . . .

I don't want/need
my eating disorder because . . .

(Here are some examples. Add your own)
_____

It makes me numb. _____

It makes me feel safe. _____

I don't feel so lonely. _____

_____

_____

_____

_____

_____

_____

It hurts my throat. _____

My heart pounds and I'm scared. _____

I don't want to be around people. _____

_____

_____

_____

_____

_____

_____

Worksheet #3
Goals Sheet

This week I will try to do the following (Examples: Talk to my best friends to find out who might be available to eat dinner with me. Write a list of activities I can do by myself to resist the urge to binge and purge in the evening. Write in my journal before and after I binge eat and purge analyzing how I was feeling before and after, where I was, what time it was, what was going on, who I was with, and what I think led to my binge eating and/or purging):

Now write your goals:

1. _____

2. _____

3. _____

4. _____

5. _____

Keep track of what you were able to do each day on each goal (Examples: Monday—spoke to Patricia. She can eat with me on Tuesday. She was so willing to help me. I am lucky to have a friend like her. Tuesday: After I ate dinner with Patricia I went home, binged on birthday cake, and vomited once. I don't know why. I never wrote activities I could do to resist the urges to binge and purge. Maybe I was lonely. I think I tried to eat with a friend too soon. I wasn't ready.)

Now write your notes for each day:

Monday _____

_____

_____

Tuesday _____

_____

_____

Wednesday _____

_____

_____

Thursday _____

_____

_____

Friday _____

_____

_____

Saturday _____

_____

_____

Sunday _____

_____

_____

Worksheet #4
What I will Do to Reduce or Resist Binge Eating and Purging

I will reduce/resist binge eating by

_____

_____

_____

(Examples: (1) I will eat dinner with Patricia on Tuesdays, Margot on Thursdays, and my cousins on Fridays. I will follow my meal plan and eat by myself at home on the other evenings. (2) I will not skip lunch. (3) I will go to my computer class right after dinner on Wednesdays. I will go to my Support Group on Monday evenings. On other evenings I will: write in my journal, do the exercises in my workbook, talk on the phone with my friends, do yoga, take a bath, listen to my favorite music, or go to a movie.)

I will use the following affirmations to help myself resist bingeing

_____

_____

_____

_____

(Example: "I can tolerate my feelings. No matter how bad they are, eating until I feel ill will not make them better.")

I will do the following to reduce or resist urges to purge

_____

_____

_____

_____

(Example: I will not go into the bathroom for two hours after I have eaten. I will always use the bathroom before meals. I will occupy myself for two hours after each meal with conversation with friends, a class or group, writing or doing exercises in my journal or workbook, doing yoga, or going to a movie.)

These are the affirmations I will use

_____

_____

_____

_____

(Example: "Vomiting is hurtful to me. It is like the abuse that I received as a child. I do not deserve to be hurt by me or anyone else.")

Daily Log (check off daily any binge eating, purging, and antecedents/circumstances)

	Binge Eating # times	Purging # times	Antecedents/Circumstances
Monday			
Tuesday			
Wednesday			
Thursday			
Friday			
Saturday			
Sunday			

When a client has successfully achieved a level of symptom reduction consistent with Maintenance for 6 months, she may need to continue to keep track of these behaviors while adding some other behaviors to monitor, such as her sexual behavior, work attendance, shopping and spending behavior, as well as desirable behaviors such as how often she is going to her support group, religious services, saying her prayers, doing yoga, or asserting herself with her loved ones or friends.

Once a client is ready for Termination, she should leave with written guidelines indicating what is a slip, and what is a fall. She should be aware of behaviors and thoughts that indicate she is slipping. She should leave with written strategies to remind her how to maintain or regain her footing. Let her know that you are available to her long-term, just like her medical doctor, if she is in need of additional support for the eating disorder or any other problem which she might face over the life cycle.

Body Image and Weight

Goals

1. To explore client's body image and weight issues and how they are impacting on her physical and emotional health.
2. To help therapists educate clients about weight-related issues and body image.
3. To teach therapists how to help clients develop a plan for a healthy lifestyle with weight as one indicator but not the only indicator of health.
4. To help therapists guide clients in developing skills and strategies to appreciate and care for the body they have.

Weight and body-image issues seem to be the major impediments to change for clients with eating disorders. Many clients no longer wish to restrictively eat or purge after binge eating, but they feel they cannot stop due to fears of inevitable and uncontrollable weight gain. Even clients who "know" intellectually that they will not gain weight uncontrollably, are terrified by the prospects of any weight gain.

Most clients with eating disorders, no matter what their size, see their bodies as fat, ugly, and out of control.

Clients whose weights are high already seem to feel it is inevitable that they will always remain obese despite their efforts and, thus, give up in discouragement and eat more.

What is this fear, obsession, and despair about weight that haunts our clients with eating disorders? Why does it hold our clients so tightly that despite their better judgement, knowledge, desire, and awareness they cannot relinquish or escape the confines of this "weighty" prison? Why is it that those whose weights are low see imaginary fat deposits where only flesh and bone exist? It seems that clients with eating disorders "wear" their weighty emotions. They "see" what others only feel. Many of them feel as if they "carry the weight of the world on their shoulders." If you explore with them what "weighs" them down, you will often find that they feel burdened with unacceptable and unbearable emotions or the real or felt sense that they must "carry" the burdens of another or many others. It's as if many clients with eating disorders feel that they cannot handle the crush of their own and others' burdens. Or, they feel that they are undeserving of a lighter load.

We've learned, through our years of work with these clients, that their weight, whether high or low, represents in physical and concrete form, the pain, anguish, terror, rage, shame, or sorrow in their lives. It is as if they cannot convey their agony, except in palpable and somatic form. Now, you might say, "I see clients whose weight is normal and still their weight obsessions and fears control them." And we would say the weight of their emotional pain haunts them like the phantom pain of the soldier whose arm was blown off in battle. It is not there physically, but the pain, regardless, is palpable and unremitting. The experience of overwhelming emotions is felt through the body . . . the body that is there, or the body that was or threatens to be there, without the ironclad control of the will, holds their pain. The will, however, has gone awry. The will to suppress overwhelming feelings has been perverted into the will to control the body. As if controlling the body through underweight or overweight or the constant refusal to allow the body the food it needs, will thwart or obliterate those feelings or lighten the emotional load. Sadly, it works very well for a while.

Deidre knew quite well how to suppress the pain and terror of her frequent encounters with her abuser. She knew that at a very low weight she ceased feeling. She knew at a very low weight she could suppress her menstrual periods and avoid pregnancy. After one pregnancy and a terrifying abortion at the age of 12, she learned well.

Anna knew that when her weight was lower, she was physically attractive to men. She had had a rather promiscuous past as an adolescent and knew when she longed for love and affection she would try to find it through sexual encounters. As a woman in her thirties, she "needed" her obesity. It repelled men. It kept her safe from her own sexual desires and longings for love and affection. It allowed her to indulge in sweets and forbidden foods, which helped her feel good, without worry about her weight gain. She was already obese and she didn't care.

Other clients don't know why they are so controlling or obsessed with their weight. They see it merely as a necessity in our weight-obsessed culture. Some recall the ridicule they received as overweight children. Some see the prejudice and hurtfulness of others' comments toward people who are overweight. They fear that this could happen to them.

Some believe that their weight will determine their success in some desired field, such as a sport, modeling, or dance. Some see it as the way to keep a straying husband or boyfriend. Some see it as the way to please or earn love or attention from a parent.

Some of these clients are right. What they experienced naturally led them to the conclusion that weight control, especially low weight, serves a protective function in day to day society. With willingness and work, most will eventually recognize that their obsession with weight has protected them from other, sometimes nameless, villains that rob them of identity, self-esteem, security, and safety.

Your task is to help your clients discover the literal and figurative meanings of their weight obsessions. The seed of this obsession with feeding the self, of eating the forbidden fruit, resides in the story of Adam and Eve. Eve ate the apple, the forbidden fruit, and was banished from the Garden of Eden with Adam. How many of your clients experience food as the forbidden fruit? How many of them fear, or have experienced real or felt banishment from others or from the self because they have eaten. How many of them say, "I don't care. I'll eat as much of the forbidden fruit as I want because I will be banished anyway?" How many of them say, "I wish to be banished, so I will eat the fruit. The place in which I reside physically or emotionally is no "Garden of Eden."

Your task is to help them discover the deeper "whys" associated with their avoidance or abuse of food. Once these tasks are accomplished, your client can decide if she wants to change her relationship with food, which typically necessitates changing her relationship with weight and her body. Are these not weighty issues? No wonder so many of our clients are riveted and frozen by weight fears and obsessions. They keep them from plumbing the depths of the weighty feelings that lurk beneath these fears. Weight is the issue and it isn't the issue. But never make the mistake of telling your client you won't talk about weight fears or obsessions with her. Let her physician or nurse focus on the numbers while you focus on the nuances. Never say you won't discuss with her why she is "feeling fat." You will never get to the weighty issues unless you address the weight issue first. Unless she deals with the "fat feeling" first, she will be unable to burrow down to the insulated feelings below. "Fat" insulates our clients from their emotional pain as blubber insulates the whale from the ocean's cold. Don't strip your client of her defense—the "fat feeling"—until she is ready.

WEIGHT AND THE STAGES OF CHANGE

Precontemplation Stage

For clients in the stage of Precontemplation, helping them learn information about weight and body image is important. Many clients do not know that weight, without extreme measures, is determined by genetics, lifestyle, age, and bone structure. Many clients do not know what normal weight is for them. They have unrealistic ideals. Many clients do not know about the scientific research concerning set-point theory and metabolism. Many clients do not know that scientific research concerning diets shows that diets are abysmal failures at maintenance of long-term weight loss. Many clients do not know about the real medical sequellae of chronic low weight and amenorrhea or the problems associated with vomiting, laxative abuse, and obesity. Since your precontemplative clients do not see their eating disorders as problems now, education within a trusting therapeutic relationship is all you can offer them. Your goal is to increase their perception of the cons of their continued behavior in hopes it may move them into the Contemplation stage of change.

Suggest that your clients review the Psychoeducation chapter in our companion client workbook. Suggest that your client read personal stories about people who have suffered with eating disorders, and that she join a psychoeducation group or a support group with people who are contemplative about changing their behaviors. The worksheets at the end of this chapter will also be helpful, as clients are ready to explore their weight and body image concerns. These worksheets will help them see how the eating disorder may be impacting on their lives even though they do not wish to change their behavior.

Contemplation Stage

For clients in the stage of Contemplation, writing a pros and cons list about the positive and negative aspects of their weight fears and obsessions or their actual weight as well as the probable positive and negative outcomes of giving up their weight-related behaviors can be most useful. It will help your clients understand and respect the reasons why they have held so dearly to theses behaviors, fears, and obsessions even in the face of declining physical, emotional, social, and cognitive health. Here is an example of Deidre's pros and cons list.

Gaining Weight into Safe or "Normal" Weight Range

Pros	Cons
I will regain my menstrual period.	I could get pregnant.
I will protect my bones from osteoporosis.	I will feel physical and emotional feelings.
I will no longer feel hungry all the time.	Without the aching hunger which controls my mind, I may think of things that I can't bear.
I can have foods that I've missed.	I will have feelings that I do not miss.
I will have the energy to run again.	I could be attacked when I run.
My boyfriend will be happy.	My boyfriend will not know that I still hurt.
I will survive.	I'm not sure I can bear to survive.

This list conveys how "protective" Deidre's low weight and obsession with keeping her weight low has been to her. She faces real fears if she decides to regain weight. However, writing these out and spending much time talking with Deidre about the pros and cons of weight gain may help Deidre understand why she needed the low weight when she was younger.

This understanding, especially if affirmed by the therapist, can help a client feel safe enough to consider changing. She does not need to hide her fears. She does not need to obscure from the therapist or herself the reasons her low weight was necessary. Should she have adequate time to address these issues, she may likely decide that she can and will change. At this point, you will need to reassure her that both of you must not push for change too quickly. First you must tirelessly prepare to protect her from all the fears associated with weight gain by developing strategies to deal with each one. Then you must work to help your client develop skills to deal with each potential fear-inducting situation as well as her internal fears. Here is where some of the work of Marsha Linehan can come in handy for your clients. Dr. Linehan has identified skills that many clients lack. Her workbook with extensive worksheets provides clients with ways to learn and keep track of their goals and skills development. Deidre and I (M. Villapiano) worked on Distress Tolerance skill building first. We refer you to Dr. Linehan's workbook (1993a) as cited in the References section of this book.

Preparation Stage

Once Deidre was ready to consider changing her low weight, we moved into the stage of Preparation. Here Deidre and I identified all the skills that she must learn and the strategies she would use to deal with her fears about weight gain. We also identified all the potential avenues of support available to help her galvanize her resolve to regain weight.

Many clients do not have, or do not solicit the support of their friends, family, colleagues, or peers. Many are embarrassed or fear if they announce their desire to change, others will be disappointed if they fail. They will be ashamed if they fail. Or, others will attempt to control them rather than support them. Still others do not trust the motivations of others. They do not believe anyone truly cares about them.

Deidre did agree to enlist the help of her boyfriend. She had feared he would no longer know she hurt if she regained weight. He needed to know of her hurt. She needed to use her words to convey her hurt. She had relied on her low weight to convey this message long enough.

Her boyfriend was thrilled to be included. He agreed to meet with Deidre and her therapist to learn how he could understand her feelings and affirm them even if she regained weight. He agreed to attend a local multi-family/friend support group for people whose loved ones suffer from eating disorders. He also asked what he could read so he could learn more. He was to be a great support to Deidre.

Deidre was afraid to tell anyone else yet. However, she agreed to see a nutritionist weekly rather than monthly to support her efforts. She entrusted her physician, therapist, and nutritionist with her fragility as they prepared for her to try change.

Here are the plans that Deidre developed during Preparation.

- Pack and eat breakfast while driving to school in the a.m. Breakfast options; bagel with cream cheese or peanut butter, 4 oz. orange juice in travel mug, travel mug of coffee.
- Listen to favorite Vivaldi or Bach tapes while eating breakfast.
- Read reasons why I need to eat lunch. Eat brown-bag lunch between 12 and 1 in student lounge. Sit near window or balcony to people-watch while eating. Write in journal for 15 minutes following eating. Write about feelings before, during, and after eating. Read all the affirmations that tell me why it was good that I ate lunch.
- Eat dinner with Jack (boyfriend). Either Jack and I prepare dinner together (from menu developed with nutritionist) or get take-out.

- Eat at table with tablecloth, flowers, nice dishes, and linen napkins. Put soothing background music on. Light candles. Engage in talk about the day. Avoid stressful or tense topics while eating.
- After dinner, sit on sofa, sip hot tea, play a board game or watch a game show on TV.
- On nights I work, arrive for shift at least 30 minutes early to give myself time for dinner. Eat one of the entrees chef prepares.
- Have cup of yogurt available for snack whether at work or home. At work, keep it on sideboard so I can take bites (between 9 and 10 p.m.) as I am able. At home, have it during study break. Tell myself I need yogurt to have the energy to meet the physical and/or mental demands of my work.
- Try to be in bed by 11 p.m. (non-work nights) and 1 p.m. (work nights).
- Write notes on progress/problems with this plan before bed.
- Write all "fat" feelings and fears . . . the literal ones and the ones that lurk beneath . . . to discuss in therapy during each session.
- Attend weekly medical appointments. Stand on the scale backwards. Dr._____ will tell me if I've lost, gained, or stayed the same. She will not give me the exact number. This is best for me because I will obsess about the number. Trust that weight is only one indication of my health. Trust that Dr._____ and my nutritionist will not let me gain weight too rapidly. They will keep me safe.

Action Stage

This was how Deidre prepared for Action. Once this plan was in place, she agreed to start it the following Monday. Jack was on board as well. He rearranged his schedule to be at home for dinner on the nights Deidre didn't work. He worked with Deidre and her nutritionist to develop a dinner menu that they could both live with. They both acknowledged the potential difficulties they might encounter, such as Deidre saying she was not hungry or she'd already eaten (frequent comments she had made in the past). Jack learned that he cannot change Deidre, nor can he make her want to be healthy. He can only be there to share dinner with her and support her efforts. Jack agreed that he would follow the dinner plan for himself even if Deidre chose not to join him. They agreed to meet with Deidre's therapist in one month to discuss how they were doing with this plan.

For those clients who do not have family or friends to support their efforts during the Preparation and Action stages of change, support groups or groups naturally available within the community can be tremendous supports for your clients. For example, find an eating disorders support group in your community or start one yourself. For clients who are involved in church or synagogue, social occasions involving eating occur frequently. Help your client become a part of these and help her elicit the help of the church/synagogue community. Help your client become involved in volunteer activities such as volunteering at a soup kitchen, distributing and sharing meals with elderly shut-ins or elderly in a nursing home. Learning to eat with people is important as is experiencing how eating with others can be both nurturing for the body and the soul. The "weight" which our clients carry can be lightened by the love, support, and sharing of others who care. If this is not available, it is amazing how support and camaraderie can grow during the process of sharing a meal with another. Help your client plan to address her weight by sharing the "weight of her world" with others.

SUMMARY

The personal vignettes in this chapter illustrate the extent of many clients' loathing for their bodies. Helping our clients see how "weighty" emotions could be, helped them appreciate the real "weight" that they carried. Over the years we have learned how critically important it is to listen to how our clients "feel fat" before they will ever feel and reveal the true weight of their feelings. From the anorexic client in Precontemplation who says her weight is fine and her body image is accurate to the abused client in Contemplation who wishes, but is afraid, to shed her "weighty" prison of fear and sorrow, clients move through the stages of change concerning their body image and weight very slowly. We recommend that you introduce your clients to the body image exercises in this book and our companion text, *Eating Disorders: The Journey to Recovery Workbook*, as they determine their readiness to address this "weighty" issue.

EXERCISE: MY BODY . . . MY SELF

Here is an exercise which clients in the stage of Contemplation have found very helpful. We call it "My Body . . . My Self." Here is a letter written by a 24-year-old client who had suffered with bulimia nervosa for 9 years.

Dear Body,

You are fat and disgusting. You have always shamed me. I remember how the other kids picked on me because of your lazy eye. I felt so embarrassed and stupid when the teacher told me to pay attention when I was paying attention; I just couldn't control your eye. Then you grew. Why did you grow so fast and out-of-control? You scared me and wouldn't let me control you. Do you know what it was like to have all the boys staring at my breasts? Do you know what it was like to have boys only want to date me to see if they could fondle those big and hideous breasts? You made me sick!

Now that I'm an adult I can control you. I don't trust you. If I give you one extra cookie you will torture me with cellulite and bulges. You disgust me.

Sincerely,
Moira

Here is her Body's response.

Dear Moira,

Do you think I wanted to have a lazy eye? Do you think I wanted you to suffer? I needed medical care. Once your mother got me the care I needed, my eye was fine. Don't you appreciate that I can see for you? Don't you appreciate that I can read for you? You love books and I have helped you enjoy this love your entire life, even when I was lazy!

As for my growth when you entered adolescence, do you think that I grew large and voluptuous to torture you? I was beautiful. Why didn't you ever appreciate me? If boys gawked it was because my beauty fascinated them. I'm sorry there was no one to help you decide which boys deserved to date you. No one helped you determine which boys would treat you with the respect and the care you deserved. I'm also sorry no one was there to teach you how to respect and admire me.

Do you know how much I enjoy helping you run? You are really good at it! These legs of mine are good and strong and agile. They have always served you well. And what about my voice? It is powerful and operatic. Everyone loves to hear me sing . . . even you.

Well, I'm sorry we haven't gotten along better. I can only ask that you treat me better now. I will serve you well . . . better than I have . . . if you'll feed me regularly and stop vomiting. It really hurts when you vomit. I really hope we can get along.

Sincerely,
Your Body

Part 1: Write a letter to your Body. Tell your Body everything you've wanted to tell it. Do not edit. When you are done, sign your name.

Dear Body,

Sincerely,

Part 2: Now, it is your Body's turn to write a letter back to you. Let your Body speak without editing. Once done, have your Body sign the letter.

Dear_____,

Sincerely,
Your Body

Once your client and her body have exchanged letters, ask your client how she felt about her letter to her body and her body's response back to her. Ask her if she developed a deeper understanding of her body. Ask her if she learned anything about her body or her self that she hadn't already known.

Over time, periodically ask your client to repeat this exercise. As she progresses, you may see these letters grow in mutual compassion, understanding, and appreciation.

The Athlete

Goals

1. To help the therapist determine whether the eating disorder is related to athletic performance.
2. To help the therapist understand the complexity of recovery in athletes where physique is equated with performance.

Drive, determination, enthusiasm, the need to please, commitment, motivation . . . these are some of the traits that help an athlete excel. Unfortunately, these are also some of the personality traits we see in individuals who develop eating disorders. The combination could be a recipe for disaster. This is especially the case in sports where physique and performance are strongly correlated, such as gymnastics, figure skating, dance, swimming, wrestling, and distance running. It is estimated that one out of every three college female athletes suffers from an eating disorder. The number of male athletes on the college level suffering from eating disorders is reportedly less, but unclear.

Some serious athletes develop eating disorders as a direct result of serious training and pressures to attain or maintain peak physique and performance.

> Annie is an example of an athlete who has developed an eating disorder as a result of her training. She began gymnastics at the age of four. What initially started out as a program in "tumbling," turned into serious training as an elite gymnast. She felt more pressure as she had gone up the ladder, competing first on a local level, and then on a national level. Annie, now 14 years old, is in the throws of adolescence. Her body has undergone significant changes. Not only has she had a growth spurt, but also she has developed curves . . . curves that Annie sees as fat and damaging to her performance. In an attempt to fight nature and maintain her athletic performance, Annie began a "diet." She would continue to eat three meals daily, but discontinued any snacking in-between meals. Annie began to lose weight, and as she lost weight she received accolades from her coach and teammates about her improved appearance and performance. This feedback encouraged Annie to continue her weight loss, but as she experienced increasing difficulty in losing more weight, she began to cut back on the amounts she ate at meals. Unfortunately, Annie's performance was not hurt by her intensified food restriction and weight loss giving her the message that continued weight loss and restriction were O.K., until it spiraled out of control and turned into anorexia nervosa.

Others use athletics to maintain and support their eating disorders.

> Ellen was a fifteen-year-old freshman high school student who tried out for the tennis team that I (Laura Goodman) had been coaching. In her first year of high school, she appeared very eager to make the team. Ellen was very slight, almost fragile, but had energy in her that was beyond belief! She was every coach's dream. I could always count on Ellen being right in front, leading the way of every practice. Her excitement, dedication, and enthusiasm were something I had wished the entire team had. On numerous occasions, I would make reference to Ellen's excitement, and use her as a role model for the remainder of the team. I knew that Ellen would

not be a starting varsity player on my tennis team, but I chose to keep her on the team, as I felt her motivation and commitment was going to allow her to improve steadily. Practices would usually end with either a one- or two-mile jog . . . a jog that was always met with tremendous resistance by the team. Ellen, on the other hand, would run the route as if she had a tremendous energy in reserve. In addition to this, I would see Ellen running home from practice; she lived approximately 3 miles from the school. What I came to learn later was that Ellen was suffering from anorexia nervosa and bulimia. She used her athletics as a way to rationalize her excessive exercise. Ellen was "training," and everyone around her became very impressed with her commitment. It wasn't until years later that Ellen was able to share that this motivation to perform was actually her way of holding onto her eating disorder.

The goal of this chapter is to help you and your clients explore the complex relationship between eating disorders and athletics. Your client athletes know the physiological and emotional benefits of exercise. Clinicians know exercise releases endorphins; these endorphins can help individuals fight off feelings of depression. Involvement in sport can also foster self-esteem. The therapeutic task is to foster balance between food and athletics. Taking away an athlete's sport can feel very punitive, and it is not always clear that it is in the person's best interest. Yet, when there are medical complications involved, there is no alternative but to temporarily stop athletics until the person becomes medically stable. Treatment should attempt to incorporate balanced athletics; however, this is not always possible. Whether and how to incorporate exercise/athletics into a client's treatment plan may be related to the client's stage of change. For example, if the client feels she has no problems with an eating disorder or over-exercise, and she is medically unstable, the physician may need to limit or prohibit exercise. If the client is prepared to make changes (move to Action) she may be able to experiment with strategies to continue her exercise with safeguards to protect from over-exercise (e.g., put a time limit on her workouts, workout with others and never alone, etc.).

Understanding the importance of sport for your client athlete will help you guide your client toward goals, strategies, and skills that will support her identity as an athlete while highlighting how her identity as a person with an eating disorder will eventually undermine her athletic performance. Explore with her the relationship she has with her coach and the role of the sport/athletics within her family. Learn from her what pressures she experiences as she excels to higher standards/levels of performance. Work with her to develop a plan to retain her athletic identity while diminishing her eating disorder identity.

ATHLETES IN THE STAGES OF CHANGE

Precontemplation Stage

An athlete in the stage of Precontemplation will be in treatment against her will. Her coach, parents, or physician have told her that she must engage in treatment in order to continue competing. She may feel backed into a corner. Sitting with a client in the precontemplative stage of change can be very difficult; sitting with a client athlete with an eating disorder can be even more difficult. For as much as you would like to work with your client to find "balance" to maintain her sport, it is often difficult to negotiate balance with a client who is in denial and/or unwilling to change. Building a relationship and providing education are key. Discuss with your client how food is fuel and how low body fuel, like low automobile fuel, means the body or car is going to come to a halt despite how hard you will it to do otherwise. Teach your clients about the impact of food restriction on muscle mass and metabolism. Your client needs to see a direct connection between care of her body and maintenance of her athletic identity and sport.

Contemplation Stage

In the stage of Contemplation, focus with your client on how she believes her eating disorder is helping her athletic performance. It can be helpful to challenge the client's perceptions, especially in regard to the areas of strength and endurance. It is not uncommon for an athlete with an eating disorder to feel good about her physical appearance while having some awareness that her physical strength and endurance have been compromised. Often the client athlete is terrified of giving up her eating disorder. She believes it has benefited her. In time, as she sees that what she thought was in her benefit is actually to her detriment, she will be more ready to find adaptive strategies to maintain her athlete status without an eating disorder. Or she may decide that she cannot, or does not want to be an athlete. It may be that she is an athlete to please another, not herself. It is at this stage of Contemplation and exploration that your client may clarify how her eating disorder has helped while hurting her.

Preparation Stage

At the Preparation stage of change, the client is increasingly aware that what she believes she is doing to help her performance is actually hindering her performance. This is the time when it will be helpful to explore with your client strategies she can employ to appropriately and accurately work toward increased athletic performance. If your client is struggling with anorexia nervosa, Worksheets #1, #2, and #4 (in Chapter 4, Understanding Hunger) can be useful in helping your client identify her hunger, develop strategies to feed her hunger, and challenge her fears around feeding her hunger. If your client is struggling with bulimia, these same worksheets can be useful. If your client has both anorexia nervosa and bulimia, all worksheets can be useful. Your client, her physician, coach, nutritionist, and you will work to develop a plan to balance healthy eating and exercise at this stage of change.

Action Stage

At the Action stage, the client needs support and encouragement. She is practicing the strategies she has learned with you to balance her eating and exercise. She may feel frustrated and disappointed . . . disappointed in herself and concerned that she may disappoint you or her coach. The frustration may stem from her belief that she must do everything perfectly. She may not know how to recover and maintain a high level of performance. She may need you and her other team members to excuse her from athletic performance until she is well. She may not be able to say she needs a break. Or she may need you and her team to tell her she may condition but not compete. You and she will discover what amount of athletic identity she needs to retain to maintain her self-esteem while also knowing that she must mute this identity to focus on her self-care and recovery. As you model compassion for her she will learn greater compassion for herself. You need to be her cheerleader; help her to continue to practice the unfamiliar and uncomfortable, and reassure her that with practice she will achieve increased comfort in her abilities. This comfort will not only be in her abilities to more easily fuel her body, but also in her recognition that proper fueling will enhance her performance and give her the strength to fight the emotional as well as physical battle of the eating disorder.

Maintenance Stage

At the stage of maintenance the client athlete's actions feel less like work and more like a lifestyle change. She is taking a long-term perspective toward her performance. She is caring for herself daily to maintain longevity in her sport rather than engaging in quick fix or short-term behaviors which will eventually interfere with or end her career as an athlete. She is able to resist the urges to restrict her intake to decrease her weight. She is able to resist the urges to binge and purge to feed her hunger while avoiding the weight which she believes will detract from her physique or performance. She is able to resist the temptation to take pills or push herself beyond her endurance and risk injury. She is able to confront coaches or trainers who condone dangerous practices for short-term gain. She is living a healthy life and eschewing all lures back to illness, even when the lure is the "promise" of heightened performance.

TEAM TREATMENT APPROACH TO ATHLETES WITH EATING DISORDERS

As a therapist, you don't want to find yourself in the punitive position of "taking away" your client's sport. Nor do you want to find yourself condoning your client's misuse of exercise as a way to maintain her eating disorder. Finding the balance can be difficult. We recommend that the treatment team develop parameters around exercise. As the clinician, you are going to be most familiar with your client's use of exercise, personality profile, and psychological issues. We recommend that you share this information with your client's physician, and encourage the physician to set the medical parameters for continued exercise. It is the role of the nutritionist to help the client explore necessary food/exercise changes to work toward maintenance of these goals, and it is your role to help your client with the psychological impact of working toward these goals (often through challenging thoughts and behaviors). When you are working with athletes with eating disorders, it is important that the coach be involved in the treatment process. This does not mean that the coach should be aware of the psychological issues associated with your client's eating disorder, but rather the coach needs to also understand the parameters for continued athletic performance, and techniques that he or she can incorporate to help the recovery process. This is critical, as it is not uncommon for client athletes with eating disorders to find loopholes in their treatment. These loopholes are ways of maintaining the eating disorder. Often we hear that people with eating disorders are "manipulative." The use of this pejorative term indicates how we misunderstand our clients. When a client finds a loophole it is her creative, and often unconscious, way of continuing to protect herself.

For example, with Annie is was important to involve her gymnastics coach in the recovery process. The coach was asked to not weigh Annie, although he did weigh all the other gymnasts. He was also asked to limit Annie's workouts and allow her to have a snack before practice, as recommended by her physician. Annie may not have relayed this information to her coach (whether consciously or unconsciously). A spokesperson for the treatment team must convey these medical requests to the coach so Annie is protected. She may not be able to protect herself.

SUMMARY

The combination of athletics and eating disorders is a very delicate and complex issue. There is no single treatment for athletes presenting with eating disorders. Restricting athletics can result in an increased state of depression and loss of self. For those presenting with eating disorders, taking away athletics can also be misinterpreted as punishment. On the other hand, allowing continued participation in athletics while struggling with an eating disorder can have permanent, and sometimes fatal results. The goal of this chapter has been to assist the therapist and client in juggling the delicate balance between the athletic identity and eating disorder treatment. As such, we have identified treatment strategies which allow for involvement in athletics as long as the client is medically stable. At the same time, we have tried to offer guidelines for helping a medically compromised client or one in denial to maintain her athletic identity even while treatment precludes her active involvement. The worksheets will take the reader through exercises pertaining to each particular stage of change. This will be invaluable for those clinicians working with both serious and recreational athletes.

WORKSHEETS

Worksheet #1 will help explore the relationship between the client's eating disorder and her sport. Worksheet #2 will help your client recognize and understand why she may fear giving up her eating disorder. This worksheet is especially helpful to clients in the stage of Contemplation. Worksheet #3 provides useful psychoeducational information to all clients. It is most useful for clients in Precontemplation, but it serves as a powerful review of the impact of eating disorders for athlete clients. Worksheet #4 will provide a form to use to facilitate ongoing communication with your client's coach.

Worksheet #1
Eating Disorders and the Athlete

1) What sport(s) do you engage in? _____
_____

2) How many hours per day do you train for your sport? _____

3) Please describe your workout:

Activity e.g., stretching	Minutes Per Day 20	Days Per Week 5
_____	_____	_____
_____	_____	_____
_____	_____	_____
_____	_____	_____
_____	_____	_____

4) What is your level of training and competition

local ___ high school ___ regional ___ collegiate ___ national ___

amateur ___ professional ___

5) Are other family members involved in sports? Yes ___ No ___

If "yes," please list the family member, sport involvement, and level of participation (e.g., recreational, high school, collegiate, regional, national, amateur, professional):

Name	Sport	Level of Participation
_____	_____	_____
_____	_____	_____
_____	_____	_____
_____	_____	_____
_____	_____	_____

6) Describe your relationship with your coach:

_____
_____

Worksheet # 2
The Role of Exercise/Sport

This worksheet may help you understand your fears of letting go of the eating disorder, as they pertain to your sport. It may also help you consider the negative impact the eating disorder will have on your athletic performance.

Write whatever comes to mind. Do not edit or judge your responses. Respond to all the sections that pertain to you.

I am afraid that if I increase my intake:

_____
_____
_____
_____

I am told that by increasing my intake:

_____
_____
_____
_____

I am afraid that if I stop my purging behaviors:

_____
_____
_____
_____

I am told that by decreasing my purging behavior:

_____
_____
_____
_____

I am afraid that if I decrease my exercise:

_____
_____
_____
_____

I am told that by decreasing my exercise:

_____
_____
_____
_____

Worksheet #3
Eating Disorders and Athletic Performance

Here are some facts about eating disorders as they relate to athletic performance.

Muscle: Fluid loss, through dehydration, can greatly decrease muscular strength, speed, coordination, and endurance. In addition, when a person is exercising, glucose is used as a source of energy for performance. Glucose gets stored as glycogen during resting times, and is replenished through the intake of carbohydrates. Very often those with anorexia nervosa restrict carbohydrates because of fear that ingesting carbohydrates will cause weight gain. As a result, glycogen will not be stored and performance will inevitably diminish.

Heart: The heart muscle will be compromised if inadequately nourished. The result will be lowered athletic performance. The effects of anorexia nervosa on the heart are: lowered blood volume, decreased oxygen utilization, smaller cardiac chamber dimensions and left ventricle mass. Strain on the heart appears as slowed or irregular heartbeat, arrythmias, angina, and heart attack.

Skeletal System: Low body weight and loss of menstrual cycle have been associated with bone loss and osteoporosis. This is due to the lack of the secreting hormone, estrogen. This permanent loss of bone density, as a result of anorexia nervosa, can result in stress fractures and other bone injuries.

Other physiological impacts of eating disorders which impair athletic performance include the following:

weakness and fatigue   low blood pressure   low blood sugar
electrolyte imbalances   iron deficiency   anemia
vitamin and mineral deficiencies

Psychological impacts of eating disorders on athletic performance include the following:

difficulty maintaining focus   increased agitation/anxiety
decreased concentration   sleep difficulties
distractibility   increased frustration with performance

Worksheet #4
Team Communication Form

This worksheet ensures clear communication between coach, physician, and other treatment providers. It is important that the client and all treatment providers and coach have a written copy of these treatment parameters to monitor follow-through and to provide clarity and safety.

Treatment Recommendations:

Medical: (e.g., client needs to have vital signs checked before workout)

_____

_____

_____

Nutritional: (e.g., client must have snack and 8 oz. of liquid, such as water or juice, before workout)

_____

_____

_____

Exercise: (e.g., client is not to work out, aerobically, for longer than 30 minutes)

_____

_____

_____

Weight: (e.g., client is able to work out as long as she is exhibiting continued weight gain)

_____

_____

_____

Other: (e.g., do not talk about weight, food, how client looks)

_____

_____

_____

Treatment Recommendations for date(s) of: _____

_____

Clinicians' signatures and disciplines

_____

_____

_____

_____

Substance Abuse and Eating Disorders

Goals

1. To help the therapist assess clients with eating disorders for substance abuse problems.
2. To teach the therapist ways to determine how the eating disorder and substance abuse may be intertwined.
3. To help the therapist determine how to intercede with the client at each stage of change.

The client with an eating disorder and a substance abuse problem presents a more complicated picture than the client with an eating disorder alone. Often, eating disorder clients are told they must attend to their substance abuse problem before they can be treated for their eating disorder. While being treated for their substance abuse problem, some clients' eating disorders are exacerbated, as the "cure" for substance abuse is calming the demons with doughnuts and cookies. Although this may calm the substance abuser without an eating disorder, it encourages the person who binges and purges to continue to binge and purge to mitigate the pain. Many clients have told us that it was easier to give up the abused substance than the eating disorder. A few reasons for this are illustrated in the following words from our clients:

> *I can stop drinking. I never have to go into a bar or a party where alcohol is served. I can live without alcohol. But, I have to live with food. If I could live without food, I would be happy, but to live with food in moderation is too much for me. (Melanie, age 20)*

> *I used (cocaine) to stop eating. Now that I'm not using I'm eating and I'm gaining weight. I can't stand gaining weight. Using is better than weight gain. (Grace, age 24)*

> *Laxatives are my preferred substance. No one even knew that they were addictive. No one knew how they were killing me, but I couldn't live without them. I nearly went into congestive heart failure trying to withdraw from laxatives. I got so fat, I ballooned to 20 pounds more than my highest weight ever. If they hadn't kept me in the hospital until the massive fluid retention receded, I would have used again. No one realizes that you're an addict when you use over-the-counter medications. But I was an addict. If I ever touch a laxative again, I know I'll never stop using them. (Lily, age 32)*

Some people with eating disorders use addictive substances to support the eating disorder, like Grace and Lily. Cocaine removed Grace's hunger. She could lose weight without effort because she never thought about eating. Laxatives gave Lily a way to minimize the effects of heavy binge eating. She could binge eat, take 60 laxatives each night, suffer profuse diarrhea, become dehydrated, and "feel" as if she had lost weight. Eventually, however, no matter how many laxatives she took, she was gaining weight.

Eventually, she gained so much rebound water weight from using and attempting to stop using laxatives, that it seemed to her the only way to lose was to increase her intake of laxatives. Only when she became unconscious and her husband had her rushed to the emergency room, did her serious laxative abuse history come to light.

For others, the connection is more subtle. Melanie did not consciously drink to allow herself to eat, but her drinking disinhibited her so she could eat. Without alcohol, she could not let herself eat.

ADDICTION

Addicted—"devoted or given up to a practice or habit or something habit forming, as a narcotic, cigarettes, etc." *Addiction*—"the state of being addicted, especially to a habit-forming drug, to such an extent that cessation causes severe trauma."

Can a person be addicted to drugs and food? The answer is yes and no. Yes, a person can be physically addicted to drugs such that they are devoted to something habit forming to such an extent that cessation causes severe (physical) trauma. Psychologically they can be addicted to drugs such that they can be devoted or given up to a practice or habit to such an extent that cessation causes severe (psychological) trauma.

A person can be devoted or given up to a practice or habit (e.g., restrictive eating, binge eating, compulsive overeating) to such an extent that cessation causes severe (psychological) trauma. Physical addiction does not occur with food because restrictive eating, binge eating, compulsive overeating, eating sugars, starches, etc., does not foster tissue dependence. Yet the psychological trauma incurred by stopping the restrictive eating, binge eating, compulsive overeating, or the reintroduction of sugars or starches, can be overwhelming. Psychological addiction can be seen in the person's need for the substance to achieve a desired effect. This effect is psychological or mental, not physical (i.e., there is no tissue or physical dependence). There is no evidence that people are addicted to food such as sugars. However, they can feel psychologically addicted to sugars or food in general.

Ginger believed, "If I eat just one bite of something sweet, I cannot stop and I'll eat until there's no more. I'll continue doing this for days because I cannot stop. So, the only solution is to never eat anything sweet." Thus, the cycle of overindulging in sweet foods followed by total abstinence of sweet foods continued. She was psychologically addicted to sweets. When asked what she associated to sweet foods, she'd say, "a treat . . . something I got only on very special occasions . . . but always accompanied by admonitions . . . 'You shouldn't really have this because you're too fat . . . but I'll let you have it just this once!'" She remembers feeling so excited when allowed a piece of cake when she was a child that she plotted to get more once her parents were asleep. She felt she could not stop. Perhaps she could not stop because she was told she could not/should not have any. As an adult, Ginger continues to plot to get sweets while continually admonishing herself for her desires. She calls this her sweet addiction. In fact she is psychologically dependent on the mental obsession of resisting and overindulging on sweets. She is not physically dependent.

Veronica believed she could not tolerate any food in her stomach once she went to bed. She would binge heavily each evening and vomit until she believed her stomach was empty. She was so dependent on this ritual that she would panic if she did not have a massive supply of food on hand, because it was only the ingestion of huge quantities of food that facilitated her vomiting. Veronica would spend the day figuring how she would get the food, how she would transport it home, where she could hide it so her roommates didn't get it, and when she could binge and purge in private. She was psychologically addicted to the purge. All of her efforts and thoughts were geared toward the satisfaction of this psychological addiction.

Evans and Sullivan (1995), in their excellent book *Treating Addicted Survivors of Trauma* wrote,

"Keeping resentments is like 'swallowing poison and expecting the other person to die'" (p. 147). Many of these clients continually 'swallow poison,' vomit it up, stuff it down, or forswear all forms of nutritional nurturance, as if it were poison. Evans and Sullivan indicate that the goal is not to "forgive and forget" but to "grieve and let go." Drinking, drugging, restricting, bingeing, overeating, vomiting, and all other forms of purging seem to be symbolic ways to drown out, starve away, and throw up the poisons of their past. Many feel these poisons exist in their very cells. *They* are the person to be destroyed. They are attacking the self, like a cancer. They do not grieve and let go except in symbol. We know that to kill bacteria we must use a potent medication. To inoculate from illness we must give a dosage of that illness. Is it possible that our clients with eating disorders and substance abuse problems are fighting poison with poison? Unfortunately, it does not inoculate. It poisons further. They are fighting the enemy, but the enemy is the self.

In the case of alcohol and drugs, if alcohol and drug usage stops, the ill effects will eventually cease. You stop taking the poison and you stop being poisoned. In the case of eating disorders, if you stop taking in food, you eventually dry up like a desert. Your body becomes a wasteland. If you take too much food, your body becomes a flood zone. Nothing flourishes in a desert wasteland and nothing flourishes in a flood. These analogies tell us that food, not too little or too much, is essential for life. Like an antidote to a poison, you need food to stay alive.

One thing we have learned about people with eating disorders and concomitant substance abuse is that the use of the substance frequently follows temporal patterns. In a study by Bulik et al. (1992) women with bulimia nervosa engaged in considerably more eating-disordered behaviors (i.e., binge eating and purging) and more licit (e.g., laxatives, diuretics, and emetics) and illicit drug use depending on the age of the participant (e.g., alcohol and cigarettes) during the evening hours. The authors suggest that the high rates of drug usage in women with bulimia may be related to the effects of food deprivation.

This premise holds some merit. Women with eating disorders often acknowledge that they smoke to decrease their appetite; they smoke to control their weight. Women who use alcohol acknowledge that alcohol disinhibits them so they eat more than they would ordinarily eat. Women who use laxatives say that they use them to compensate for the food they've eaten. Again, this is a weight-control technique.

In a beautifully documented conversation with Rachel V. (1987) (the pseudonym for a well-known author in recovery), Marian Woodman (1987), a noted Canadian psychoanalyst, says people who are addicted to alcohol are "longing for spirit because they are so mired in matter, but they make the mistake of concretizing that longing in alcohol." She goes on to question, "What is this terrible starving in an addiction? It's as though our whole civilization is feeding the hunger, not to satisfy, but to make us hungrier. There is this sense of "I want more, more, more of—something. In eating disorders—bingeing, anorexia, bulimia—you find the same drivenness. Addicts do their best to discipline themselves and they may do a very good job from 7 am to 9 pm. Then they go to sleep. Their ego strength goes down and suddenly the unconscious comes up. As soon as the unconscious with all its instinctual drive erupts, the ego loses control. Then the addiction becomes a tyrant. Its voice is that of a starving, lost child: 'I want, I want, I want, and I am going to have.' There's an instance of the weak confounding the strong" (p. 146).

Rachel V. then says, "I don't know that much about anorexia and bulimia except they seem to be akin to some kind of profound rejection of the body" (p. 146). Marion Woodman replies, "Yes, a profound rejection of matter."

We interpret this to mean that the person with an eating disorder and a substance abuse problem does not want to live in this world. She is rejecting the body and mother earth. She is profoundly rejecting matter. Powerful feelings such as love, hate, anger, shame, sadness, loss, frustration, terror, and disappointment have become concretized in the body. They are too intolerable to bear emotionally. Bodily, in the form of matter, they can be controlled, squelched, or annihilated with over eating or restricting, purging, or dulled or drowned in drug or drink. These feelings, so unbearable, have left the emotional realm and are felt in the body. The body, burdened by the enormous weight of such feelings, likewise, wishes to rid itself of these feelings. Alcohol and food numb the feelings of body and soul. The person escapes this world. She neither feels nor experiences her feelings . . . her humanness. The alcoholic hates feelings and washes them away. The person with an eating disorder hates "fat," the embodiment of these hated feelings, and attempts to numb them, stuff them down, or expel them by virtue of some purging technique.

TWO CASE ILLUSTRATIONS

Case 1: Mia

Having stopped drinking for 6 months, Mia told of the feelings she had for a love that was not reciprocated. She said, "I felt that all my worst fears had been confirmed. I am fat, ugly, disgusting, and unlovable. I feel as if someone ripped my heart out and stamped all over it. My first inclination was to walk to a liquor store. I took a walk and didn't even intend to go to the liquor store, but my feet took me there. Starving, binge eating, and purging don't help enough. I needed alcohol to escape my pain."

Mia, like so many other people with eating disorders, feels her feelings in her body. She attempts to reject her body to reject her feelings. She also interprets her feelings as a confirmation of the ugliness of her body. If another does not love her, she must be "fat," she reasons. She rejects her body (and feelings) and believes others feel as she does.

So, how are you to assess and assist your clients with eating disorders and substance abuse problems? Firstly, remember, readiness to deal with one symptom does not mean readiness to deal with another. Your client may tell you she's sick of dealing with the after-effects of drinking, but she may be loathe to give up her eating disorder.

One year ago, Mia came to the conclusion that she had to stop drinking. She had been going on drinking binges for three months. Her job demanded high-level, sensitive, security measures. She needed to be very discrete, sharing very little about what she did with others. One evening after a full night of drinking, she awoke in the bed of a man she did not recognize. She had no money in her pocketbook and she did not recognize where she was. She panicked. She could be at risk for losing her job. Had she had a blackout? What had she done with her money, or had her money been stolen? She was already late for work. She had a very important meeting to attend and she would not make it. She called her friend who worked in the same company. The friend told her she needed help . . . that her drinking was out of control and she was at risk for being found out at work. Terrified that all these things were true, Mia finally admitted she had a drinking problem and agreed to check herself into a detox program. She was not saying for sure, "I never want to drink again," but she was saying, "if I don't break this cycle right now I might lose everything I've worked for." She would change short term (e.g., not drink while in detox), but would she change for good? She needed to stop drinking and work at the stage of Contemplation to address whether or not she was ready to stop drinking. She needed an opportunity to look at the pros and cons. She knew the pros, the "why I should not drink" list, quite well, but needed to fully understand the cons, the "why I still want to drink" list, better. She needed to decide if she was ready to change.

She was not ready to change her eating disorder. She was in Precontemplation. She knew that the eating disorder was not good for her, but it had not caused her such serious problems that she wished to change. She liked being thin and she liked the feeling of emptiness in her stomach. The emptiness and the purging helped unburden her of unbearable feelings. She was not ready to give this all up.

This client is ready to work on the drinking problem. This problem takes precedence. Right now, she is motivated and the impetus to change is great. If she were in Precontemplation about her drinking (as she was before this last blackout) she would have said, "I do not have a drinking problem." In Contemplation, she is saying, "I know I have a problem, and I want to change but I am afraid. What will I have to face, feel, and do if I'm not drinking? What else must I give up, if I give up drinking?" She must contemplate these questions before she can prepare to change. She is not ready to contemplate these questions with her eating disorder. At this time she is not experiencing such severe consequences around her eating disorder. For example, she can keep her binge eating secret. No one needs to know that although she eats very little during the day, she binges all night. No one needs to know that she vomits each night before bed. She does not need to prepare to change her eating. But, the potential negative consequences of drinking are so great right now, that she is more ready to contemplate the pros and cons of drinking. She is more ready to prepare to change this behavior now.

How does the therapist help a client change a behavior she is ready to change (in Mia's case, her substance abuse), when that behavior is psychologically connected to a behavior she is unready to change (the eating disorder)? The answer lies in the stages of change. Mia needs help understanding the connection. She might benefit from reading the Bulik article (Bulik et al., 1992). Having adequate information about what drinking can do to her, as well as how her drinking and eating problems may reinforce each other might help Mia move from Precontemplation around her eating disorder to Contemplation where she is with her substance abuse disorder. Clearly, however, she is more ready to change her drinking behavior because she has begun to experience consequences that frighten her.

If your client is in Precontemplation suggest that she read about eating disorders and alcohol dependence and learn how they may interrelate. Learn how one may encourage the other and vice versa. The Bulik article (Bulik et al., 1992) as well as the chapter on substance abuse in our companion book, *Eating Disorders: The Journey to Recovery Workbook*, offer very useful information to clients who are abusing substances.

If your client is in Contemplation, encourage her to write a pros and cons list about drinking or drug use. What are the reasons to stop drinking or using drugs (the cons of drinking or using drugs)? What are the benefits (the pros of drinking or using drugs)? How would not using substances change your life for the better? For the worse? How would not using substances affect your eating? How would not using substances affect others?

Mia's task was to work on this "decisional balance" as described by Prochaska et al. (1994). She needed to do an exhaustive assessment of the pros and cons of changing her drinking behavior before she would be ready to move onto Preparation. Because changing drinking can have an impact on eating, clients with eating disorders who also have substance abuse problems are often reluctant to address the substance abuse problem. They fear giving up the abused substance will lead to increased or uncontrolled eating and weight gain. To attempt to minimize their concerns or push them into premature action around the substance abuse problem is generally unproductive. Firstly, premature action often leads to failure, disappointment, and, sometimes, terror. Clients stop drinking but become even more symptomatic with their eating disorder. They are unprepared to deal with these changes, so they either begin to abuse the substance again, or they become increasingly panicky, depressed, or engage in even more self-destructive behavior (e.g., cutting). Therefore, it is important to thoroughly assess the consequences of giving up their substance abusing behaviors as they relate to their eating disorder. Only when this is done in great and exhaustive detail, do clients embark on the preparatory efforts to stop their substance abusing behaviors, but they may also begin to contemplate reducing their eating-disordered behaviors. For example, when Mia understood that not eating all day lowered her resistance to abstinence from alcohol, she was willing to consider increasing her daytime eating. She was not willing to give up her eating disorder, but she was willing to provide herself with a bit more sustenance to shore up her abstinence efforts. Reading about the physical, emotional, and cognitive impact of restrictive eating, binge eating and purging by vomiting as well as the physical, emotional, and cognitive impact of alcohol abuse helped to increase Mia's resolve to work on both problems. She was able to begin to see the pros, or benefits, of abstinence from alcohol as well as the benefits of increased daytime eating.

What we have learned is that a head-on approach to an eating disorder is not always the wisest approach. By this I mean, addressing Mia's restrictive daytime eating itself would have had less of an impact on her readiness to change than would addressing her restrictive daytime eating as a factor which encouraged alcohol consumption. Restrictive daytime eating alone was not a problem for Mia. Restrictive daytime eating that encouraged alcohol consumption, however, was a serious problem which Mia wanted to change.

Case 2: Vicki

Here is another example of how to help a client work on her eating disorder and her substance abuse without a direct attack on either.

Vicki was a first-year law student. She worked all day and attended law school at night. She was determined to earn her degree despite the financial stresses and time demands of working full time and going to school. Vicki also had a serious eating disorder (bulimia nervosa) which included abusing laxatives. Vicki was in the stage of Contemplation concerning her eating disorder. She knew it was a problem. She hated that she binged and purged by vomiting, but she didn't mind her restrictive eating. In fact, she liked it and wished that she could always eat restrictively. She didn't like taking laxatives, though, because they made her feel quite ill. She had become so dependent on laxatives that she feared what would happen if she didn't have a constant supply on hand to counteract the effects of her nighttime binges.

As I (M. Villapiano) asked her about her laxative usage, I learned that Vicki was so ashamed of her heavy usage that she had taken to stealing the laxatives from a variety of local pharmacies and convenience stores. She was shoplifting almost daily to support her habit. Interestingly, she also shoplifted because she did not want to pay for something that ultimately "ended up in the toilet." Yet, she could not fathom giving up her laxative habit. She was convinced she would become obese because she was certain she could not control her extreme binge-eating habit.

It became clear that Vicki was in Contemplation about parts of her eating disorder (her binge eating and vomiting) and her laxative abuse, which, though part of her eating disorder, was as well a substance abuse problem. Although in Contemplation about these problems, once we talked about the legal ramifications of the shoplifting should she get caught, Vicki's entire demeanor changed. It was as if she had been struck by lightning. An "a-ha" had occurred. She was able to say, "I may not be ready to give up using laxatives, but I could never tolerate being arrested for stealing them. I had never thought before about the ramifications it could have on my legal career. Could I be admitted to the Bar with a shoplifting conviction on my record?" I said that I did not know, but that I was sure it would not enhance her application.

It was at this moment that Vicki propelled herself into the stage of Preparation around the laxative abuse. She wanted to know how to stop immediately. Portraying the devil's advocate, I asked if she had truly contemplated what she would have to face, do, and feel without the laxatives (i.e., she was clearly seeing one of the pros of change but had she considered the cons of change?). Vicki did not think this was so important at this time. In keeping with her impulsive and intense approach to life in general, she was ready to impulsively propel herself into a "no laxative" life. Now, we should be overjoyed, should we not? At last she has seen the light! No! Vicki is taking the easy way out. She is not ready to stop, because she does not understand the consequences. Therefore, the chances of failure and discouragement are great. How will she handle it if she steals the laxatives anyway? What will she do without the laxatives?

I suggested that we consider how to go about this in a more measured way. I asked how she would feel about using laxatives, but only if she bought them? I told her I thought it was premature to stop them entirely because she had not contemplated, nor prepared for, the consequences. She became pensive, remarked at how paradoxical my approach was, as her former therapist admonished her for using laxatives at all. She said, "Dr. X would have cheered if I had told him I wasn't going to use laxatives anymore, and you're telling me it's too soon to stop! I like your approach better. It makes me feel less pressured and more hopeful." I remarked that research told me it was the better way.

Vicki began, that day, to reduce her laxative consumption dramatically. She had been taking 4 to 8 laxatives almost every evening. Now, to avoid shoplifting and to conserve money, she began taking one per evening. She wanted a box to last her almost a month. I told her the month would give her time to consider the pros and cons of stopping her laxative abuse totally. If she decided to stop completely, we would then move to the Preparation stage of treatment and draw up strategies and work on developing skills to help her abstain from laxatives. Within 3 months, Vicki was no longer using laxatives. Three years later, Vicki is still laxative-free.

We took a multi-part approach to prepare Vicki to reduce and then abstain from laxatives.

First, we looked at how to get the environment to support her efforts. How could we do that? We realized that the temptation and opportunity were greatest in stores that sold laxatives. So, Vicki planned to avoid stores as much as possible. To do this she needed not only the resolve to stay out of stores, but some means of purchasing other things she needed from these same stores. She decided she would enlist her mother's help. Vicki's mother was always willing to help, but Vicki was always reluctant to ask for help or give her mother any idea about how to help. This time Vicki agreed to fill her mother in. She told her mother that her goal was to reduce her laxative usage and asked her mother if she would shop for her toiletries and sundries so she could avoid these stores. Her mother agreed and Vicki agreed to give her mother a certain amount of money each week to cover these purchases.

Second, Vicki needed help to stay away from these stores. Walking by them alone was a temptation. Shopping and stealing had become a lunch-hour ritual. She would buy her binge foods, steal her laxatives, and call that her lunch hour. Now she needed something else to do during that hour. What could she do? Having lunch, which makes sense to us, was more than Vicki could do. But, she thought, maybe she could buy and eat a bagel. She had done this before. She usually felt fairly safe with a bagel and it was easy to buy only one. Then she thought she would need to find something to do. Eating a bagel alone would make her too anxious and tense. She decided that she liked people-watching. She knew of some very nice areas where she could take her bagel, sit on a park bench, and watch the lunchtime crowd pass by. It was summer; the weather was beautiful and she knew the fresh air and sun would also help her feel good. Therefore, that was her plan.

In her rush to eliminate the chances of an arrest (as she wanted to be a lawyer), she became contemplative and began to consider preparations to work on her eating and laxative usage behaviors. Sometimes, recovery requires re-framing the goal. It always requires searching for the behavior that the client really does want to change. In Vicki's case, I could have told her that she must stop laxative abusing. I could have told her how at-risk she was medically from this abuse. Had she been in the stage of Precontemplation that information could have been helpful to her. However, re-framing the goal as "protection from arrest for shoplifting so I can be a lawyer" was the goal that resonated with Vicki. It moved her to seriously contemplate the pros and cons of laxative abuse, and in her wish to reduce this behavior she began to prepare to address her eating disorder as well.

Vicki's preparations included: asking her mother to buy her toiletries and sundries; giving her mother a fixed amount of money each week to do this (this included money for one package of laxatives per month); walking a different route during her lunch hour to avoid the temptation to enter pharmacies and convenience stores; identifying a bagel store and walking to it each lunch hour; buying one bagel; finding a great people-watching spot to sit and eat her bagel; and returning to work without walking the pharmacy/convenience store route.

Vicki kept good written records of her efforts each day so we could determine how she was doing. Soon she was ready to act. She was already acting around her eating and laxative reduction, but she wanted to act to totally stop laxative usage.

Within 3 months, she told her mother she was no longer going to ask her to buy a package of laxatives. She told her mother she decided to stop altogether. She had had plenty of time to determine the pros and cons of no laxative usage at all. She had decided that the decisional balance supported no laxative usage. She had already established a supportive structure for avoiding stealing, and thus, reducing her laxative usage. She felt the next step was within her reach. She had come to realize that laxatives reduced her anxiety and fear. At first she thought it was just about weight gain. Then she realized it was a calming pill. Laxatives told her she could relax. She didn't have to worry any more. She would be ok. She didn't know how else to calm herself, although she realized that restrictive eating, binge eating, and vomiting also helped to calm her. How else could she calm herself? We began to prepare a "calming" plan that she could try in her efforts to stop calming by use of laxatives. She wrote down everything she thought might calm her that was not also dangerous. She agreed to ask her family, friends, and colleagues how they calmed themselves. She read about relaxation techniques. She tried massage and tai chi. She kept track of everything she tried. By the end of 3 months, she had devised a list of 10 things she could do to decrease her anxiety and thus her urge to use laxatives. She agreed to practice at least 2 of these daily. They became her new rituals. Instead of stealing and using laxatives each day, she went to church, either the dawn Mass or the early evening Mass. She carried her rosary beads and did the rosary every lunch hour after her bagel and people watching. She took her dog for a walk each evening before bed and really looked at the stars and the moon, admiring them and allowing herself to marvel at their awesomeness.

She entered the Action stage after 3 months of Preparation. She practiced these behaviors religiously. She did not slip again into laxative abuse, and has been laxative-free for 3 years. She is not free of her eating disorder, but it is better. At some point, I hope she will be ready to say good-bye to her eating disorder as she has bid adieu to her laxative usage.

At this point, however, she and I can look at her progress and say, she did change one problematic behavior. She vigilantly works at maintaining this goal each day. Someday, I hope the strength she has derived from this accomplishment will give her the faith in herself to know she does not deserve to be eating-disordered anymore.

SUMMARY

In this chapter we have looked at physical and psychological addictions and the ways in which restrictive eating, binge eating, purging, and substance abusing can intensify and mutually reinforce each other. Through clinical case examples, we saw how the use of licit and illicit drugs and alcohol can make someone with an eating disorder feel more in control of their eating or not eating. Finally, we see how exclusive treatment of one disorder without support and treatment for the other often leads to relapse or the exacerbation of symptoms in the untreated disorder.

As in other chapters, helping clients identify a reason to change leads to more efficient movement through the stages of change than targeting the behavior alone. For example, in Mia's case, she did not want to stop abusing laxatives. They helped her deal with her intense fear of weight gain. However, she did not want to be arrested for stealing laxatives, so to achieve that goal, she limited her laxative use.

Treating clients with eating disorders and substance abuse disorders requires that therapists identify each client's stage of change for each disorder. Even if the client is in different stages of change for each disorder, the therapist must try to find a way to weave change in one disorder with change in the other. Suggesting that clients read information supporting how one disorder may intensify and support the other can help clients at the Precontemplation stage as well as all other stages of change.

Sexual Abuse and Eating Disorders

Goals

1. To help the therapist determine how best to assess clients with eating disorders for sexual abuse.
2. To demonstrate how to assist clients in working on sexual abuse issues at their stage of change.
3. To help the therapist become familiar with treatment issues and techniques useful to all clients with a combined eating disorder/sexual abuse history.

Working with the client with an eating disorder who has also been sexually abused requires patience, gentleness, and the ability to tolerate hearing horrifying and, sometimes, terrifying details of abuse. These clients, like many who have been abused, may not tell of their abuse upon first meeting with you, even if you ask. They may not know they have been abused. They may have some confusing memories that may indicate that something uncomfortable happened to them but they may not be sure it was abuse. Or they may know they were abused, but believe that divulging such sordid, awful, or painful details would cause them greater pain, shame, or humiliation, especially if they are not believed. Some may have been silenced by threats.

Research results indicate that victims of sexual abuse do not readily or easily divulge their abuse histories to their therapists (Pribor & Dinwiddie, 1992). A study done at the Renfrew Center, a residential treatment facility for those with eating disorders, found that only 30% reported sexual abuse histories on the intake questionnaire, yet 61% divulged a history of childhood sexual abuse during the subsequent interview (Miller, 1996). Miller found that inverted-funnel questioning versus funnel questioning appeared to yield higher levels of reporting of childhood sexual abuse. The questioning differs in the following ways. Funnel questioning is broad questioning: "Have you ever been sexually abused?" This type of question can be shocking and can demand too much of a reluctant client. Inverted-funnel questioning, such asking, "Do you recall feeling uncomfortable with the way someone touched you when you were a child?" is gentler, less shocking, and requires less of the reluctant client. It does not require the client to quickly search her memory for possible abuse and then decide that it was abuse in order to answer the question in the affirmative. If she is a client in Precontemplation, she does not want to be in your office anyway; therefore, she likely would not answer in the affirmative and she would find your questioning further off-putting. Therefore, the first critical ingredient in assessing the eating disorder client for a possible history of sexual abuse is to ask, gently and non-threateningly, about such a history using inverted-funnel questioning.

A second critical ingredient needed is the establishment of a positive, trusting therapeutic alliance. Although important for all clients, for clients with eating disorders who have histories of abuse, the experience of a trusting, abiding connection with the therapist is the second essential ingredient needed for the client to report her abuse history. The client must be shown through the sensitivity and directness of the questioning in the first session that the therapist knows that sexual abuse may be part of the experience of the client with an eating disorder. Her comfort in saying that many people with eating disorders have had uncomfortable, disquieting sexual experiences as children prefaces why she is asking the client whether she has had such experiences.

The asking alone is an indication to the client that the therapist knows about sexual abuse, is comfortable asking about it, and, therefore, can tolerate hearing about it should it be reported. As Judith Herman (1992, p. 148) states, one of the central therapeutic tasks of the therapist is to "listen and bear witness." The therapist must unambiguously convey that she can and will be able to tolerate hearing about "unspeakable" atrocities (p. 1). Should the client bravely begin to speak such unspeakable truths, the therapist must show in her demeanor and words her ability to weather the horrors of the client's private storm.

ADDRESSING ISSUES OF SEXUAL ABUSE IN EACH STAGE OF CHANGE

Precontemplation Stage

The client who enters the therapist's office in Precontemplation about her eating disorder may be precontemplative about revealing abuse issues as well. Clients who present with multiple symptoms of bulimia nervosa such as binge eating, vomiting, and laxative abuse, as well as those with many other risk-taking or self-injurious behaviors such as sexual promiscuity, kleptomania, substance abuse, and self-mutilation, are likely to have been victims of abuse. Others with seemingly less complicated presentations may also have histories of abuse; however, the former client may benefit from a more thorough explanation of how eating disorder symptoms are protective in nature.

In other words, educating clients in Precontemplation about how eating disorder symptoms initially came about to protect and defend the person from unbearable feelings is the task. Then let the client know that all the other risk-taking or self-injurious behaviors she is engaging in also came about to protect her from unbearable feelings or experiences. Remark about her enormous strength and ingenuity in finding all these ways to keep the unspeakable, unbearable pain from overwhelming her. Let her know that her strength and ingenuity will serve her well if and when she is ready to find another solution to this unbearable pain. Her eating disorder and all these other self-abusive behaviors, once all she had, are now destroying her along with the pain of her abuse. Reassure her that when she is ready, you will help her find another way while embracing and honoring her enduring strength and ingenuity.

For a client without such a multiproblem presentation, it is enormously reassuring to have a general, comfortable talk about the purposes the eating disorder serves and how important it is to acknowledge and respect how the eating disorder has helped her, before deciding that she deserves a kinder servant. Many suddenly perk up and wish to explore more. Some reveal their secret wish to be rid of the eating disorder despite their belief that they could not live without it. These are the doors that, if opened, beckon the client to step to the next level of change, Contemplation.

Contemplation Stage

For the client in Contemplation, there is an acknowledgement and recognition that the eating disorder is hurting her, yet she knows it protects her from the unbearable pain of the abuse. She may be so terrified of the feelings, thoughts, or memories of the abuse, that she cannot contemplate giving up the eating disorder or other self-abusive behaviors for fear such feelings or memories will annihilate her. Yet, she does contemplate it for she has allowed herself to know the eating disorder is hurting her.

This client can be helped by concretely chronicling the ways in which the eating disorder hurts and the ways in which it protects, specifically as it relates to the abuse history. This is the stage where it is useful to explore the abuse history in as much detail as the client can tolerate. The client needs to know that you want to hear, and can tolerate hearing, all the information she can share. Ask such questions as:

- Who was the abuser?
- How old were you when you were first abused?
- How long did the abuse last?
- Were you abused by more than one perpetrator?
- What was your relationship to the abuser or abusers?
- Did anyone else know or should others have known?
- What amount of force or threat was involved?
- How did you understand the abuse then?
- How do you understand the abuse now?
- Have you told anyone in the past? How did that person(s) react to your telling?

All are difficult but important questions for you to ask the client. Following this line of questioning, ask the client the following set of questions:

- When do you believe the eating disorder first started?
- Did it coincide with the first instance of abuse or threatened abuse?
- Did the progression of the eating disorder stop the abuse or reduce its severity or intensity?
- Did the eating disorder help you escape the pain, terror, or anguish of the abuse?
- Was food or alcohol forced on you or otherwise used on you as part of the abuse cycle?
- Was food or drink the reward for going along with the abuse?
- Did vomiting, starving or bingeing help you numb yourself from the abuse or the memory of the abuse?
- Did low/high weight repel the abuser?
- Did low weight and cessation of menses protect you from impregnation by the abuser?

A "yes" to any of these questions should prompt you to ask, "Might this be one of the ways the eating disorder has protected you?" Likely, the client will say "yes."

Once you have all of the information about how the eating disorder helped her, tell her how understandable it is that she is ambivalent about saying good-bye to her protector/tormentor: her eating disorder. Tell her how you see that the eating disorder, though hurting her now, was her salvation. Tell her how you will work tirelessly with her to help her find a long-term, adaptive, non-abusive, and doable solution to coping with such a painful history. Tell her if she could tolerate and live through the abuse, she can tolerate and live through the difficulty of saying good-bye to and grieving the loss of the eating disorder symptoms, because now you and she understand why they had to be there.

Once she is ready, it is time to move onto the task of chronicling all the ways in which the eating disorder hurts her. Help her look at all the quadrants of her life by asking such questions as:

- How does it affect school/work? Specifically, look at your performance, output, evaluations, attendance, concentration, focus, energy level, communication, and interactions with fellow students or coworkers.

- How does it affect your home life/social life? How are you interacting, communicating with your family members/roommates/friends/lovers? How are you socializing with them? Are you sharing meals or activities? Has your involvement/interaction/communication with your family/roommates/friends/lovers changed over the course of your eating disorder?
- How does it affect your personal care and functioning? Describe your sleep patterns, eating habits, elimination, sexual functioning, grooming, and hygiene.
- How does it affect your spiritual life? Do you have a relationship with a higher power/God? Has that relationship changed? If so, how?

A client who answers these questions and hears you acknowledge and affirm her strength and wisdom at finding a way to survive her abuse is suddenly free to begin to grieve the loss of her eating disorder as she prepares to cope more directly and adaptively with her pain. When she is ready to take the next step, she will move to the stage of Preparation.

Preparation Stage

The client who is in the stage of Preparation is ready for change, but she does not yet have the ability to successfully change. She does not have the tools, resources, structures, and supports she needs to effect change. She needs to carefully plan her attack. Plan A alone is not enough. She must not go into battle alone and unshielded.

Operationally, this means you must work to help your client develop the skills and amass the tools necessary for conquest. She must now learn to predict with you what barriers and landmines she might face. She must learn to outwit and exhaust the eating disorder in its quest for victory over her healthier, life-seeking self, especially as the abuse memories and feelings emerge. She must learn how to support and sustain her efforts to face and tolerate her abuse memories and feelings while being seduced by the forces of the eating disorder which urge her to vomit, starve, or binge eat to keep abuse memories and feelings at bay. Here are some of the tools and coping strategies that have helped others with eating disorders and abuse histories successfully prepare for this battle.

EXPRESSIVE/EXPERIENTIAL TECHNIQUES

Journaling. Write a dialogue between the eating disorder and healthy self. The following is an excerpt from one of our clients:

Eating disorder: Just eat one more, it will take away the pain. Keep stuffing it in. It will help you sleep and then the pain will be gone.

Healthy self: I need to feel it and face it. If I eat to stuff it down it will just be there again when I wake up. And then I hate myself for the abuse and for the bingeing. I doubly disgust myself. I'll hurt for the abuse, but I'm tired of hurting for you.

Eating disorder: You won't be able to sleep if you don't eat. You know you'll lie awake all night. You know the flashbacks will terrorize you. Come on just eat one more. It always helps!

Healthy self: You always tell me to eat just one more. You make me sick and tired. You want me sick and tired and zombie-like just like my abuser did. Then I didn't cry or scream or complain or tell how he hurt me over and over and over again. I won't let you do this to me anymore!

The pain will never stop until I stop you and my abuser from abusing me anymore. Stop! No more!"

Write a story about your child-self.   Find a picture of yourself as a child. If you don't have one, find a picture of a child in a magazine or watch a child playing at a park and write what you would feel for this child if you knew she was being abused. What would you have done to protect this child from abuse? What do you feel for this child? Would you have this child binge, purge, or starve to tolerate the abuse? Keep this story with you. Read it daily, especially at times when you are at risk for listening to the eating disorder when the pain of the memories is greatest.

Affirmations.   Write affirmations to help you remember to care for yourself when stressed, scared, or overcome by abuse memories. Keep these affirmations with you at all times. Read them when you wake up, eat, take a break, ride on the bus, get into bed, and brush your teeth. Read them at least 10 times a day. Post them on your bathroom/bedroom mirrors, post them on the dashboard of your car, carry them in your wallet on an index card, write them in your journal, put them in the top of your lingerie/under-wear drawer, jewelry box, desk drawer. Save them on the desktop of your computer. Send them to your most trusted friends and ask them to e-mail them to you everyday. Here are some affirmations that our clients found helpful:

- My body deserves gentle, compassionate care from me even if others never treated it that way.
- Abuse is wrong. It was wrong for _____ to abuse me. It is wrong for me to abuse myself.
- Starving my body, forcing my body to eat too much, forcing my body to do without the nourish- ment it needs by vomiting or abusing laxatives is abusive. My abuser "starved" my body of lov- ing care and respect, forced my body to accept abuse, and purged me of the belief in my good- ness and myself by defiling me. Abuse is wrong in any form.
- I could never hurt a child. I am that child.
- Would I ever tell (e.g., a child, my sister, my daughter, my son, my cat, etc.) she/he must go without food, stuff him/herself until ill with too much food, or vomit what he/she eats because he/she was abused? Never!
- I must soothe my hurting heart.

ARTISTIC EXPRESSION

Draw, paint, or make a collage depicting the eating disorder's response to the abuse and the healthy self's response to the abuse. Compare and contrast them.

MAKE A LIST OF ALTERNATIVE, ADAPTIVE WAYS TO COPE

Write a list of all the things you will try to do when the urges to engage in eating-disordered behaviors/ thinking are likely to overwhelm you. We compiled this list from our clients. Have your client add her own unique coping strategies.

1. Write in my journal at least 15 minutes. Do not stop. Do not edit.
2. Listen to Vivaldi's *Four Seasons* with headphones.
3. Visualize myself taking my abuse memory(ies) and locking them in a beautiful, antique chest, locking the chest in an antique store in town and going back home. Only I have the key. I will open it when I'm ready.
4. Call my friends, _____ and _____. Talk until I feel better. If they're not there, listen to their voices on the answering machines and remind myself what they would tell me if they were there.

5. E-mail my trusted friends, _____ or _____. Write until the urge to eat, restrict, or purge abates.
6. Brush my dog. Remind myself that his love and devotion for me are boundless and unconditional.
7. Take a walk (unless it is dark). If it is dark, sit on my porch and rock in my rocking chair.
8. Take a shower. Gently wash off the terrible feelings and let the caring feelings in.
9. Look at a picture of my sister. Would I treat her this way?
10. Read my old journals. Remind myself of my progress. I can hold on!
11. _____
12. _____
13. _____
14. _____
15. _____

SUPPORTS

No one should go into battle alone. So, part of your client's preparation must include helping her find a support network. Who should be included in this support network? A support is anyone who can and will support your client's efforts to choose self-care over abuse. A support is anyone who can and will listen. You and your client must discuss whom, within your client's circle of family, friends, coworkers, neighbors, etc., your client could go to and for what. If your client has no one, you and your client must work to fashion a support network. In every community there is a network of support. You just need to find it. Look for resources within churches and synagogues, hospitals and clinics, or the 12-step network. There is support available. These support networks may not automatically, or ever, be the places where your client may talk directly about the abuse or the eating disorder. Nevertheless, if your client finds a place of mutual caring, unitary focus, and commitment to some common goal, she will feel the support and she will be steeled in her efforts at recovery. That support will buoy her when she feels herself sinking into the abyss of the eating disorder and abuse.

Case examples of support networks.

> Sarah could not feed herself. Eating was noxious and painful. She lived alone, ate alone, cried alone, and was almost always frightened alone. She studied long and hard for she was completing her third year of medical school. She walked miles each day lugging a heavy book bag. She slept too little, never rested, and was eternally frightened that her heart would give way and she would die. Yet, she still could not eat.
>
> When she came to me (M. Villapiano) she resisted any intervention that would include other people. She did not want to include her parents in her work. Although they were several hundred miles away, they would have come. She did not want to include any friends. Although she was very lonely there were one or two friends in whom she felt she might be able to confide. Yet, she refused.
>
> At last, she told me about her connection with her church. She loved and admired her minister from afar. She went to the minister's evening teas whenever she could. She had once sung in the choir, but was having trouble staying connected. Along with two friends, this was her support network.
>
> After much discussion, she spoke with her minister, who had been quite worried about her, and gave her minister and me permission to speak. Her minister wanted to help but knew she could not be her lifeline. Sarah and the minister decided they could always sit next to each other at tea. This gave Sarah the feeling of support and care that she needed. The choir director called Sarah and invited her back in. Sarah went and the director periodically called Sarah just

to say "hello" and see how she was doing. Occasionally they would meet for lunch. Finally, she began to meet for coffee or lunch with another woman in the choir whom she admired. This support network helped Sarah move from Preparation to Action. She found, once she felt connected and cared for, she could eat with these people. What brought them together was their mutual commitment to their church and their music. This connection and mutuality gave Sarah the means to practice nurturing her body and soul.

Genevieve had suffered with an abusive, alcoholic father and then with an abusive, alcoholic husband. She felt worthless, stupid, and hopeless. Food was her only consistent source of nurturance. She could count on nothing else. Suffering from knee joint pain, high cholesterol, and angina, Genevieve knew if she did not learn to stop compulsively eating to assuage her pain, she would become disabled by her crushing weight and medical complications. Like many other women with eating disorders, she was alone in her eating and in her suffering. She had tried every diet program. Even if she lost weight, she soon regained it and more.

    We took a different approach. I told her she was too alone and we must find her a support network. She had always believed she was alone except for her psychiatrist who saw her for 15 minutes per month to adjust her medication. We talked about 12-step programs. We talked about Al-Anon and how it might be a place to talk about how her father's and husband's alcoholism had affected her. I told her she might find solace and support in hearing from others that struggled to live with alcoholics. After 6 months of gently exploring this and other possible support networks, Genevieve went to a meeting. After 3 months, she accepted another woman's offer to sponsor her. A year later, Genevieve meets her sponsor once a week. They go to lunch and to a museum or a concert. They have gone on retreats together and her sponsor is ever available to talk by phone when Genevieve feels herself unable to cope. For the first time, Genevieve is eating healthier and losing weight very slowly. She is walking a bit each day, planting flowers in her yard, and letting herself rest now and then.

Genevieve's support network, like Sarah's, helped her move from Preparation to Action. Finding a support network and enlisting these supports as the soldiers in her battle for recovery, as well as the development of the battle recovery plan, propelled each of these women into action . . . the active doing of battle to overcome the eating disorder and the legacy of abuse.

Action Stage

The client in Action is the client actively engaged in battle. She has prepared her battle plans. She has the tools, resources, strategies, and structures necessary to wage a successful battle. Plus, she has her support network . . . the soldiers in her battle. She is not fighting alone.

    This client is making forays into a scary world—eating in restaurants with family or friends or sharing meals with coworkers or classmates. She is alone in her house late at night fighting the urge to binge, purge, or starve away her terror as the abuse memories envelop her. She is trying to tolerate the discomfort and panic of a rounder stomach . . . as she is now eating and not taking laxatives. She is using her coping strategies, calling her supports, and practicing her affirmations.

    From you, she needs the encouragement to continue practicing even when she sees herself as "failing." She needs to hear from you that all the coping strategies and affirmations and supports that she has decided to use may or may not help her. We tell our clients that everything we try is an experiment. Experiments are ways of proving or disproving a hypothesis—an educated guess about an outcome. If we prove the hypothesis true (i.e., the outcome is as expected) or if we prove it false (i.e., the outcome is not as expected) we yield valuable information. In short, we collect data. This data or information is useful whether or not our hypothesis was true or false.

    Our task as clinicians is to help our clients see that all attempts at a solution are valuable. Therefore, none are failures. Should the coping strategies, affirmations, or supports not help the client at a particular time, instead of letting her decide she has failed, we need to say to the client, "Let's go back to the drawing board and come up with some ideas. We have learned something valuable from this. Should we try something else? Did we give this enough time? Are we looking to do too much too soon? Have you any other ideas? There is always something else to try! We will come up with something. You have not failed. You have tried and trying augurs success."

Your task as the clinician is to generate hope, fight discouragement, affirm the client's efforts, and never give up. You must believe in her when she cannot believe in herself. You must help her subdue the voice of the eating disorder while amplifying the healthy, life-seeking voice. Here is one case example.

> Vanessa used to vomit when the flashbacks became overwhelming. It calmed her. Now, diligently, she practiced her coping skills: writing in her journal, reading, watching "mindless" TV, calling her sister, taking a shower, and listening to classical music. She was making excellent progress. She was keeping more and more food down and regaining weight. She felt proud of her efforts to reduce her vomiting but she hated gaining weight.
>
> One night, following a very stressful day when the flashbacks were particularly cruel and unremitting, she agreed to go out with friends, where she drank heavily. When she returned home, she did not vomit; but, unable to stop the viciousness of the nightmares, she cut her wrists with a razor blade. Seeing the blood soothed her, but eventually, even in her drunken haze, she knew she needed help to stop the bleeding. She paged her therapist who assessed her level of risk, called the police, and had her taken to the emergency room where she received 23 stitches to close her wounds.
>
> The next day, when she and her therapist spoke, Vanessa struggled to contain her shame and sense of failure. She felt she had lost all that she had gained. She was without hope. They reviewed all that she had done over the past year. Her accomplishments were numerous and remarkable. However, both agreed never vomiting was not as important as never cutting herself and never drinking. They went back to the drawing board and looked at what might help the next time the flashbacks and nightmares were so vicious and unremitting. They decided three things: 1) She should call one of her supports or page her therapist if she was feeling, or was worried she could be feeling, this badly as the evening approached; 2) She would inform her closest supports that she could not drink and that she needed their help not to be in drinking environments especially when she was stressed; and 3) She and her therapist would need to analyze what had happened in detail to see if they could figure out at what point the first danger signal should have been heeded so they could muster a better offense next time. In other words, they needed to be able to better predict what had pushed her to the precipice of self-destruction so they could keep her far from the edge, protected, and safe next time.
>
> Although Vanessa had been solidly in the stage of Action concerning her eating disorder she needed to retreat to the stage of Preparation, where she and her therapist would develop a plan to assure her safety on her journey to recovery.

Maintenance Stage

The client in Maintenance is the client who has mastered Action. She is the client who no longer vomits to occlude the memories of abuse. She is the client who has regained weight and can tolerate sexual feelings and the renewed interest in sex without starving herself. She is the client who has been able to gradually shed her weighty armor and forego food when she is racked with feelings of shame and self-loathing.

Sadly, once clients have reached the stage of Maintenance, supports tend to drop away. They and others feel their need for support has diminished as your client's success has grown. Truly, they do not need the same kinds of support, but they still need support. Although they may be in the stage of Maintenance regarding their eating disorder, they may be in the stage of Contemplation regarding the abuse.

They are ambivalent about relationships, particularly intimate relationships. They may ask themselves, Is it safe to be intimate with another? Do I know how to choose a good partner? Will I find someone else to abuse me? Will he leave me once he learns I have been abused? Am I damaged goods . . . not worth another's love or care? Can I ever have a healthy sex life? Do I want a sex life?

Many clients who have made excellent progress overcoming their eating disorder, need to go back to the stage of Contemplation with you to address relationship and intimacy issues. If you can do this with your client, she will feel held through the next stage of her recovery process. If she is not ready to embark on this journey with you, move back to the stage of Precontemplation with her. Use your time with her to educate her about relationships if she is willing to stay. If she is not, say your good-byes and let her know you will be ready and willing to embark with her on the next leg of her journey when she is ready.

TRACKING WORKSHEET FOR CLIENTS WITH MULTIPLE SELF-DESTRUCTIVE BEHAVIORS

For clients with eating disorders, abuse histories, and histories of other self-abusive behaviors, the following chart can help you and your client monitor target behaviors. As with so many of these clients, keeping track of multiple behaviors can be overwhelming for them and you. Therefore some form of charting or tracking, like the following can be enormously helpful. Clients of ours who have been trying to reduce multiple self-destructive behaviors while trying to increase self-care behaviors keep charts like this one to follow daily. We review it each time we meet.

The headings can change dependent on issues you and your client are targeting for change. The following is an explanation of the chart as it relates to the behaviors that Carlin is targeting for change.

Carlin is tracking whether or not she took her medications (Meds) in the prescribed amounts. She indicates whether she ate her meals and snacks (B,L,D,S), whether she purged (Purge) and how much she slept (Sleep) each evening. Since sexual promiscuity and alcohol usage have been problematic for her, she keeps track of whether she engaged in sexual intimacies (Sex) or whether she drank alcohol (Alcohol). She rates the strength of her urges to self-mutilate (Urges) and whether or not she has acted (Actions) on those urges. She keeps track of how miserable she is feeling (Misery) and how successful she was in practicing positive thoughts (Affirmations).

This method of charting and tracking behaviors has helped Carlin report on behaviors she has considered shameful without having to talk about them in each session. She pulls out the chart each time she and her therapist meet and thus, with less anxiety, lets her therapist know how she is doing. This charting system also offers Carlin and her therapist the opportunity, over time, to observe subtle changes, to see progress, to predict a crisis, to ward off crises, and to work more proactively toward her goals. This method of charting has made the therapy and the in-between session time more effective and productive. Feel free to copy this chart for your clients. The first one is a sample with examples. The second one is blank for your use.

Daily Log

Name: Carlin   Week of: 10/22/99

	Meds (type/dosage)	Eat* (B, L, D, S,)	Purge (Yes/No)	Sleep (hours)	Sex (Yes/No)	Alcohol (type/amout)	Misery (1 = None; 10 = Extreme)	Urges** (Intensity: 1 = None; 10 = Extreme)	Actions** (Yes/No)	Affirmations (Practiced: Yes/No)
Mon	150 zoloft	D,S	No	4	No	None	3	2	No	Yes
Tue	150 zoloft	B,L,D,S	Yes	4	No	None	4	3	No	Yes
Wed	150 zoloft	D,S	No	4	No	None	4	3	No	Yes
Thu	150 zoloft	D,S	No	3	No	None	5	4	No	No
Fri	None	No	No	2	Yes	5 Beers 6 Shots of Whiskey	8	8	No	No
Sat	150 zoloft	S	Yes	2	Yes	Pint Vodka	8	9	Yes	No
Sun	None	No	Yes	0	No	None	8	9	No	Yes

*Eat: B = breafast; L = lunch; D = dinner; S = snacks ** Refers to *Self-destructive* Urges and **Actions**

Daily Log

Name: Week of:

	Meds (type/dosage)	Eat* (B, L, D, S,)	Purge (Yes/No)	Sleep (hours)	Sex (Yes/No)	Alcohol (type/amout)	Misery (1 = None; 10 = Extreme)	Urges** (Intensity: 1 = None; 10 = Extreme)	Actions** (Yes/No)	Affirmations (Practiced: Yes/No)
Mon										
Tue										
Wed										
Thu										
Fri										
Sat										
Sun										

*Eat: B = breafast; L = lunch; D = dinner; S = snacks ** Refers to *Self-destructive* Urges and Actions

As you can see, working with the client with an eating disorder and a sexual abuse history frequently means you and your client will need to pay attention to symptoms and behaviors which will emerge as the eating disorder abates. Sometimes these problematic behaviors exist already. It requires a delicate balance and shifting focus to help a client decrease her eating-disordered behaviors while keeping other self-destructive behaviors in check. Helping the client focus on her general safety is important. At times her safety will be more compromised by her eating disorder and, at other times, other self-destructive urges or behaviors will threaten her safety more. Keeping her safe may mean tracking, but putting less emphasis on eating and purging behaviors. At other times eating or purging becomes the greatest threats to her safety and must be focused on exclusively.

Working with the client with a sexual abuse history requires more time, patience, compassion, and fortitude from you and the client. You and she will determine how to pace your work and keep her safe as she journeys toward change.

Nutritional Counseling

As with our other specialty chapters, this chapter (though geared toward the nutritionist), can be quite useful to other treatment providers. This is especially the case in circumstances where nutritionists are not available to be a part of a treatment team. For example, some rural communities may find the closest nutritionist is many miles away. Therefore, it may not be feasible to include a nutritionist as a part of the treatment team. There may also be occasions where insurance companies will not cover nutritional services, and the client does not have the means to pay for such visits. It is for reasons such as these that we also recommend the therapist review this chapter and educate herself on nutritional counseling. If you are a therapist that does not have access to a nutritionist, or if you have clients who are unable to see a nutritionist (as a part of the treatment team) we recommend that you work closely with the physician to set up a nutritional plan.

THE HISTORY OF THE FOOD PYRAMID

Numerous studies have found a link between nutrition and health/disease. Every day we are learning more about foods, which, if lacking in the diet or overused in the diet,can contribute to disease, as well as those that can help prevent disease. Society's quest for health does not stop here. The search for the "perfect" diet, and the pursuit of thinness has helped the American diet industry become a multibillion-dollar industry. That's right! We are spending billions of dollars every year to lose weight; yet the antithesis is happening. We are becoming fatter and fatter! Such information usually terrifies people with eating disorders. Some fear they are, or will be among the fattest people in our society. Many do not know what is and isn't true about food and diet ads. Many feel that all information is relevant to them, or heed information that is irrelevant to them. For these reasons, the nutritionist offers people with eating disorders valuable information and support. She alone can help those who suffer with eating disorders distinguish between all the food and weight-based information that is and is not relevant to them. She can help them develop a plan that is unique and correct for them.

In order to address society's quest for health, in 1992, the U.S. Department of Agriculture (USDA) developed what is now known as the food pyramid (Shaw, Fulton, Davis, & Hogbin, 1996). Its purpose was to target issues of health, diet, and disease and illustrate what constitutes a healthy diet. It had two goals as its focus. The first goal was a nutritional goal; the food pyramid would determine a healthy diet. This included outlining healthy amounts of protein, vitamins, minerals, and fiber, while urging moderate calorie consumption and the sparing usage of fat, saturated fat, cholesterol-rich foods, sodium, added sugars, and alcohol. The second goal was a "usability" goal. The focus here was to provide a practical and easy to read plan for consumers to follow in their quest for healthy living. In the food pyramid, foods are grouped by nutrient content and how they are used in meals. Serving sizes are acknowledged, as well as variability of needs (based on sex, activity level, and age). Finally, the food pyramid guide allows for flexibility so consumers can choose foods that fit their lifestyle and tastes.

This approach does not encourage dieting. Instead, it encourages sustainable lifestyle change. We all know that diets do not work; the food pyramid tries to provide a lifestyle change that will be more apt to result in long-term health benefits. Finally, unlike the "four basic food groups," the food pyramid acknowledges and allows for the consumption of fats. It does, however, encourage that fat intake be no more than 30% of total calories.

The food pyramid branched off from the "four basic foods groups" because it found that although the concept of the "basic four" helped people understand nutrient needs, it didn't establish guidelines for nutrient adequacy or excess consumption. The information that has formed the food pyramid is based on the Recommended Dietary Allowances (RDA) endorsed by the Dietary Guidelines and by consensus reports of authoritative health organizations. The guide was developed for Americans who eat from all five food groups. Certain groups, such as vegetarians, specific cultural groups, and those with specific medical conditions should consult with a nutritionist to make sure they are able to obtain and sustain dietary health.

Unlike the "basic four," the food pyramid acknowledges different caloric needs for different people. As such, it helps determine serving choices based on needs. If an individual needs more servings than the minimum (on the food pyramid), servings are suggested, along with modest increases in fat and sugars (which reflect the increase in consumption). Increasing amounts of grains, fruits, and vegetables helps increase caloric intake, while continuing to maintain moderate levels of fat and sugar.

When determining a meal plan for your client, a variety of factors needs to be assessed. These include: (a) family traditions (the culture of the family, the family's relationship with food, etc.), (b) family diet history, (c) food choices and patterns, (d) school and/or work schedules, (e) activity level, (f) age, (g) gender, (h) personal health issues and/or concerns, and (i) family history of medical concerns/issues. Below you will find a chart that generalizes caloric intake needed for certain populations. Please note that this chart is a generalization; specific recommendations should be made on an individual basis. At the end of this chapter you will find numerous worksheets that we hope will help you educate yourself and your client on healthy eating.

THE THREE CALORIE LEVELS WITH SERVING RECOMMENDATIONS

Calorie level	**1,600 calories** Approximate servings for sedentary women, and older adult sedentary men.	**2,200 calories** Approximate servings for children, teenage girls and active women.	**2,800 calories** Approximate servings for teenage boys, active men, and very active women. Pregnant & breastfeeding women may need more.
Bread group servings	6	9	11
Fruit group servings	2	3	4
Vegetable group servings	3	4	5
Meat group servings	5 oz.	6 oz.	7 oz.
Milk group servings	2–3*	2–3*	2–3*
Total fat grams ~	53	73	93
Total added sugars (tsp.) ~	6	2	18

*Pregnant or breastfeeding women, adolescents, and young adults (up to 24) need 3 servings.
~Total fat and added sugars includes sugars that are naturally in foods, as well as fat and sugars from oils, fats, and sweets.

THE HISTORY OF NUTRITION COUNSELING

Kathy King Helm, RD, LD, states that nutritional counseling began more than twenty years ago, when society entered the "Wellness" era (Helm & Klawitter, 1995, p. 3). It was at this time that we began to encourage individuals to take responsibility for their own nutritional and health needs. People were choosing to receive nutritional counseling, despite the lack of coverage by insurance and government funding. This response changed the expectations of the nutritionists. No longer were they having only one or two visits with an individual, as they were accustomed to while working in an inpatient setting. Instead, they found themselves meeting with individuals on a more frequent and longer-term basis, in order to more completely address the concerns at hand.

In the past, nutritionists gave their clients "diet" plans or meal plans that would address their individual needs. Through experience nutritionists learned that providing their clients with meal plans was not enough; meal plans did not increase motivation or readiness for change. Psychological factors needed to be addressed in order to produce change. Nutritionists who wished to help people address the psychological issues which impeded change as well as nutritional issues, began to include psychological theory and practice in their education. The role of the nutrition counselor was becoming increasingly defined. "Diet" would no longer be the sole focus or topic between the nutritionist and her client. Instead, a relationship and understanding of psychological concepts was needed to effectively explore the issues that were hindering nutritional change. The nutritional counselor's role would ideally include the following:

1. Assessing clients' nutritional needs and having a solid understanding of food related health concerns (such as diabetes, hypertension, heart disease, eating disorders, family history, etc.) and recommended treatments.
2. Determining individual clients' current nutritional plan, weight, and caloric intake. Using this information to help establish a healthy nutrition plan, set-point weight, and appropriate caloric intake.
3. Providing appropriate and relevant education on nutrition and on clients' particular health concerns. Included in this would be information on: set-point theory, metabolism, genetics and family history, the purpose of food, the concept of hunger(s), body weight versus body fat, exercise, and the relationship between food and mood. Whenever possible, offering educational materials and/or resource lists to supplement verbal information.
4. Communicating recommendations to physician and/or other treatment providers. It is imperative that each team member has an understanding of their role, and the role of other providers. Be cautious not to overlap and make certain the team provides consistent messages to the client.

The nutritional counselor is an invaluable member of the treatment team. If a nutritional counselor is available to work with your clients, this is what she will be. Although you may have heard that "eating disorders are not about food," if food is ignored, you are not providing your client with appropriate care. The nutritionist will acknowledge your client's food issues and concerns while helping her understand that feeding herself adequately will provide the foundation for recovery.

An adequately nourished client can use her cognitive skills in therapy (and maintain medical stability). Without adequate nourishment, clients often languish in therapy, unable to process information or concentrate. The nutrition counselor supports therapy by helping those with eating disorders appropriately and adequately nourish themselves.

Typical nutrition goals for those with anorexia nervosa are (a) to increase food intake and weight, (b) differentiate "hungers," (c) challenge restrictive behaviors (and purging behaviors, if present), and

(d) "legalize" food. For those struggling with bulimia or binge eating disorder, nutrition goals might be to (a) maintain a healthy weight, (b) differentiate "hungers," (c) challenge binge and/or purge behaviors, and (d) "legalize" food. For all clients with eating disorders, nutritionists discuss the role of exercise and help modify exercise behaviors, as necessary.

The initial interview, like the initial therapy interview, may set the stage for a good working relationship. Many clients will walk into your office with anxiety and uncertainty. They will be critiquing and absorbing every detail of your office, and you. As we have suggested in Chapter 2, Therapist Issues, please make your office and yourself "eating-disorder friendly." That is, avoid messages and attire that focus on or reinforce dieting, thinness, food, and weight (for more information, please refer back to Chapter 2).

In general, our clients have told us that the nutritionist is the "least threatening" treatment provider. He or she is spared the role of enforcer, as the physician sets weight goals and will decide if the client needs to be hospitalized due to low weight, and the therapist encourages the client to explore underlying issues. Both of these treatment team members push the client's envelope of safety and comfort. The nutritionist is there to help the client devise a meal plan that will help her maintain or gain weight as per the medical contract with her doctor. Sometimes clients feel a certain safety with the nutritionist not felt elsewhere. They can talk about food (one of the client's favorite, yet most stressful topics), and they don't need to delve into the issues beneath the food. For these reasons, the nutritionist is experienced by many clients as the treatment team member who offers refuge. If this occurs for your client, encourage this supportive and safe relationship and acknowledge to yourself how difficult it is to implement eating goals—an area associated with both physical and emotional discomfort for your client in her relationships with her physician and therapist.

Although clients with eating disorders may feel safety in the relationship with the nutritionist, the powerful psychological factors associated with eating disorders can make the work of the nutritionist more difficult with this population than with others seeking nutritional counseling. Working with clients with eating disorders in psychotherapy can also be uniquely challenging for the psychotherapist. Therefore, the more each professional on the treatment team understands the roles and goals of the other, the more likely the team will work together to support the client and each other.

THE THERAPIST'S NUTRITION ASSESSMENT

Determining who should be present at the initial nutrition assessment is as important as the information to be gathered. If the client is a child of 13 years of age or younger, you may want to initially ask one or both parents (or the child's guardian) to attend the initial meeting, or at least part of it. For those 14 and over, we suggest that you initially meet with the client alone, and then ask the parent(s) or guardian to join the two of you toward the end of the meeting. For those under 14, a meeting of this type can be frightening; having a parent present can ease anxiety. For those 14 and over, meeting alone can provide safety, trust, and empowerment for the client. This is not a hard-and-fast rule. There may be younger children who want to meet alone initially, and older children who may want a parent present. If you are unclear about who should attend the initial meeting, we recommend that you ask the client if she has a preference.

Once you have determined who will be present at the initial meeting, your next step is to begin the evaluation. The focus of your initial assessment should be on:

- history of eating patterns
- history of weight
- history of attitude and beliefs about food

- history of family relationship with food, diet, and weight (including cultural relationship and experience)
- history of treatment (both past and present)

At the end of the chapter is a sample Nutrition Assessment form. Once completed, present your recommendations as you conducted your assessment. That is, if the initial assessment involved the client and parent(s) present, we suggest that your recommendations be presented to the client and parent(s). If, however, you initially met with the client alone, we recommend you share your recommendations with her before sharing with her parents. It may be helpful to talk with your client about how best to present the recommendations to the parent/guardian, as the client will still be critiquing every move you make. How you present your recommendations to your client's parents/guardian may determine how safe and trusting the client feels with you. By this we mean that if you break confidentiality, or talk to the parent as if the client is not present, or report something the client asked you not to say, the client will not trust you or feel safe with you. As in the therapy relationship, the relationship the nutritionist has with the client must be carefully crafted to foster safety and trust.

Once you have completed your assessment and made a diagnosis and recommendations, the next step is to devise a treatment plan with your client that will help her feel safe and minimize her anxiety while helping her move toward greater health. For example, a client with anorexia will be afraid of any weight gain, so you can tell her that you'll devise a plan for her that will help her gain slowly. You will promise her that you will monitor her weight gain with her doctor so if she gains weight too quickly, you will revise your meal plan. For the bulimic client who binge-eats on sweets each day, you might help her introduce "safe" foods into her daily meal plans before demanding that she incorporate her riskiest binge foods. Your job is to help your client achieve greater health and well being at a pace and with a plan that she can tolerate. If she must be pushed, do so gently, compassionately, and with a constant desire to minimize her anxiety and fear throughout the process.

Whether or not your client is ready for change, she should be connected with a treatment team. Do not allow yourself to be the sole provider, as eating disorders are serious psychiatric disorders, and need comprehensive treatment. Beginning with the initial stage of treatment, tell your client what professionals are on a treatment team and insist that she be in treatment with others as a stipulation of your continued work with her.

NUTRITIONAL ISSUES ACROSS THE STAGES OF CHANGE

Precontemplation Stage

If your client is in the stage of Precontemplation she is either denying that there is a problem, or she is meeting with you under duress. The goal of this stage is psychoeducation. In particular, the goal for the nutritionist at this stage is to teach your client about the risks associated with eating disorders. At this first stage, establishing a relationship and creating a safe atmosphere can help the reluctant client move to the next stage of change. Safety and the establishment of a caring, warm, and understanding relationship will help soften reluctance. The additional goals of this particular stage for you are to provide nutrition education, and education about how eating disorders impact on physical, emotional, and cognitive health and wellness. It will be important for you to assess your client's knowledge of these topics and to clarify any myths. Worksheets #1, #2, #4, and #5 will help you provide your clients with relevant psychoeducation about themselves and food. All of your clients could benefit from this psychoeducational material, but those in Precontemplation benefit from education the most, as they do not yet see the eating disorder as a problem.

Contemplation Stage

Clients in the stage of Contemplation are aware that the eating disorder is a problem, yet they are terrified of giving it up. They are aware that change is going to mean eating in ways which will make them feel uncomfortable. For example, clients who think any fat in their diet will make them fat will need to hear why some fat is needed in their diet. I know clients who changed their eating behaviors once they learned how their body fat content compared to that of elite female athletes. Claire, a 20-year-old female client with anorexia nervosa, dramatically changed her eating behavior when she learned that her body fat content was lower than that of elite female athletes. She was amazed that not only could she not build muscle, but that she was using muscle for fuel to keep her alive. She did not have enough body weight or fat, nor was her diet substantial enough to provide her with other sources of fuel. Once she had this information, she was better able to assess the reasons why including some fat in her diet made sense even though it still frightened her. She also explored with her nutritionist the least anxiety-producing ways for her to add fat.

Another client had never eaten an orange. She was 24 years old. She had been raised to believe that fruit juices were "nothing but sugar." Juices were not kept in her home and on the rare occasion when she was offered juice at a relative's or friend's home, her mother instructed other mothers to "cut the juice in half with water" to reduce how much sugar her daughter ingested. She extended that information to all fruit. Therefore, she would only rarely allow herself to eat any fruit, and never fruit which she believed could be made into juice.

Her nutritionist explained to her why fruit, and some juice, was good for her. She learned about vitamins and minerals and the benefits of roughage. Although she was terrified of including these foods in her diet, she was better able to weigh the benefits as well as the psychological drawbacks of including fruit in her diet.

No one is better able to help clients face their concrete fears of food. The nutritionist can offer substantial help to the client in the stage of Contemplation as he or she, more than other team members, can counter faulty beliefs and myths about food, and support clients' efforts to look at the pros and cons of adding, increasing, or reducing certain foods in their diet. Worksheets #2 , #3, and #4 are useful for clients in the stage of Contemplation.

Preparation Stage

In the stage of Preparation, a specific plan of action gets created. The nutritionist helps the client develop the meal plan after looking at all the options. For example if the goal is to add fat to the diet, the nutritionist and client have already looked at how to best do that by addressing the pros and cons of adding fat during the stage of contemplation. They have also looked at the least anxiety producing way to add those fat grams. When Claire progressed to the stage of Preparation, her nutritionist decided that the best way for her to add fat was by adding low-fat yogurt and 2% milk to her diet. Although Claire was frightened, she agreed to the plan. The nutritionist, like the therapist, told Claire that this would be an experiment. If it worked (i.e., if she could increase her fat consumption this way) that would be great. However, if it didn't work, they would look at other ways to add fat to her diet. Interestingly, after several plans, Claire decided that she would prefer to add fat by eating her favorite cookies, Oreos, and going back to fat-free yogurt and skim milk.

During the stage of Preparation, the nutritionist and client predict and seek solutions to potential problems. Sometimes it requires referring back to psychoeducational information such as reviewing "what it takes to gain a pound" when clients are struggling to take a bite of a cookie. Worksheets #2, #3, #4, #5, and #6 will come in handy during this stage of recovery.

Action Stage

The stage of Action is the stage where the practicing occurs. This is where the new eating plans are practiced. It is at this stage that the client uses the skills and strategies that she developed in the previous stages to execute her plan.

Action is the active doing of the plan. It is the trying on of new behaviors. It may not facilitate change immediately. You and your client will need to be patient. Some of what you try may work. Some may not. Whatever the client tries will yield useful data. You and she will learn what to change and what to leave the same. Her actions may bring about change that is temporary or change that is enduring over time. She may have slips and revert to old behaviors. The trick to preventing a downward spiral of relapse is to help your client recognize that sometimes slips can teach us important things. You and she will revise plans or use new strategies to accomplish goals. Most importantly, your client needs to learn that a slip is a lapse, not a relapse, and that she will regain her foothold on change if she goes back to the action plan rather than seeing the slip as a defeat and reverting to old behaviors in discouragement. Reminders of strategies developed in earlier stages as well as alternative plans can help her deal with lapses. The ultimate goals in the Action stage are to: (a) normalize eating, (b) identify and satisfy physical hunger, and (c) work toward lifestyle changes. Develop action goals with your client that she can practice between sessions. As she becomes more and more confident of her ability to meet her action goals, you and she can decide to decrease the frequency of your appointments.

Maintainence Stage

The stage of Maintenance is an extension of the Action stage. It is at this stage, however, that change is beginning to occur with decreased effort. This is what is referred to as a lifestyle change. Reinforcement and acknowledgement of personal strength is key. Identifying natural shifts in thought processes, feelings, and behaviors are important. What once felt unimaginable is now becoming a reality. For example, Sheila, a 22-year-old woman, no longer eats restrictively. She plans her meals in advance, packs lunches and snacks to take with her when her school and work schedule are especially tight, and she closely monitors her exercise and intake. She meets with her nutritionist about once a month now. Usually they review how she is doing with her meals in light of her busy schedule. They also review her exercise and intake. Her nutritionist helps her focus on problem areas. For example, Sheila recognized that when she is feeling guilty she "forgets" to eat. Her nutritionist reviewed some educational material with her and they developed a plan to eat "on schedule" no matter what the circumstances or her feelings. They reviewed how past experience told them that "forgetting" meals had led Sheila to bouts of serious depression and decreased her resistance to drinking. They looked at normal, consistent eating as an antidote to depression and substance abuse. Sheila still needed these contacts with her nutritionist to help her "see" and address issues which she could not see alone.

At the stage of Maintenance, the nutritionist helps the client codify the belief that "food is just food," to remove it from the realm of emotional problem-solving, and to highlight how maintaining a consistent, normalized eating plan will steer her toward emotional, as well as physical well being.

For further readings and worksheets on this topic, please refer to the companion client workbook, *Eating Disorders: The Journey To Recovery Workbook.*

SUMMARY

In this chapter, the importance of the role of the nutritionist as a part of the treatment team was addressed. Although not always possible, incorporating a nutrition counselor as a part of the treatment team is important for recovery. For those that don't have access to nutritional counseling, the therapist should work closely with the physician to set up a nutritional plan. As such, this chapter is not solely for nutritionists, but for any team members interested in learning more about nutrition counseling as a part of recovery.

This chapter provides education on the current use of the food pyramid and the history of nutrition counseling. In addition to this, there are tools and strategies for establishing treatment goals and conducting the initial assessment. Finally, it addresses the determining factors associated with treatment planning, and how to share these recommendations with the client. As with the other chapters in the book, these recommendations are based on Prochaska's stages of change theory, and are summarized as the following:

1. Precontemplation: Provide education on eating disorders, associated risks, and the pros of change. At this stage, it is also important to create a safe and non-threatening environment for the client.
2. Contemplation: Help the client face their fears of food; challenge faulty beliefs and myths; and support the exploration of the "cons" of adding, increasing, or reducing certain foods.
3. Preparation: Help with the development of a meal plan after exploring the fears stated above.
4. Action: Encourage and support the client as she begins to practice the strategies needed for change.

Following the guidelines above can yield positive results and recovery to those struggling with anorexia, bulimia, or binge eating.

Nutrition Assessment

Date: _____

Name: _____ D.O.B. _____
Address: _____
_____

Phone: (h) _____ (w) _____
Emergency Contact: _____ Phone: _____
Current Weight: _____ Height: _____
Desired Weight: _____ Highest Weight and Date: _____

Family History:
Mother's Name: _____ Age: _____
Father's Name: _____ Age: _____
Sibling Name(s): _____ Age(s): _____
_____ Age(s): _____

Does anyone in the family have a history of weight issues (including extended family)? If so, whom?
_____
_____
_____
_____
_____

Does anyone in the family have a history of eating disorders (including extended family)? If so, whom?
_____
_____
_____
_____
_____

Does anyone in the family have a history of diabetes, high cholesterol, high blood pressure, or heart disease (including extended family)? If so, whom?
_____
_____
_____
_____

Food History:
What are your binge foods (if applicable)?
_____
_____
_____
_____

What are those foods that you are afraid to eat (if applicable)?

_____
_____
_____
_____
_____

What foods do you dislike (genuinely dislike; not related to the eating disorder)?

_____
_____
_____
_____
_____

Do you have food allergies? If yes, what are your food allergies, and what is the reaction?

_____
_____
_____
_____
_____

(For those who eat restrictively) What methods of restriction do you use? Circle all that apply:

restrict carbohydrates	restrict fats	restrict calories	skip meals
restrict protein	restrict calcium	restrict snacks	restrict meals
go on fad diets	other (explain) _____		

(For those who purge) What methods of purging do you use? Circle all that apply:

vomiting	laxatives	diet pills	exercise	starvation
diuretics	other (explain) _____			

What is your current typical daily intake?
Breakfast: _____
_____
Snack: _____
Lunch: _____
_____
Snack: _____
Dinner: _____
_____
Snack: _____

What times of the day do you eat your meals and/or snacks?
Breakfast _____ A.M. Snack_____ Lunch _____
P.M. Snack _____ Dinner _____ Nighttime Snack _____

Where do you eat most of your meals and/or snacks and with whom?

_____

_____

_____

_____

_____

Please circle how you currently feel about your body:

strongly dislike   dislike   slightly satisfied

satisfied   very satisfied

What are your nutritional goals?

_____

_____

_____

_____

_____

Clients' presentation: _____

_____

_____

Recommended caloric intake: _____

Educational needs: _____

Nutritional needs: _____

Emotional needs: _____

Behavioral needs: _____

Readiness for change: _____

Recommendations: _____

_____

_____

_____

_____

_____

Additional comments: _____

_____

_____

_____

_____

_____

Date of next appointment: _____

Signature: _____

Worksheet # 1
Self Analysis Quiz

With permission from ANRED (Anorexia Nervosa and Related Eating Disorders, Inc) we have included the following questionnaire. Please circle the items that depict your feelings and/or behaviors.

1. Even though people tell me I'm thin, I feel fat.
2. I get anxious if I can't exercise.
3. (Females) My menstrual periods are irregular or absent.
   (Males) My sex drive is not as strong as it used to be.
4. I worry about what I will eat.
5. If I gain weight, I get anxious and depressed.
6. I would rather eat by myself than with family or friends.
7. Other people talk about the way I eat.
8. I get anxious when people urge me to eat.
9. I don't talk much about my fear of being fat because no one understands how I feel.
10. I enjoy cooking for others, but I don't usually eat what I have cooked.
11. I have a secret stash of food.
12. When I eat, I'm afraid that I won't be able to stop.
13. I lie about what I eat.
14. I don't like to be bothered or interrupted while I'm eating.
15. If I were thinner, I would like myself better.
16. I like to read recipes, cookbooks, calorie charts, and books about dieting and exercise.
17. I have missed work or school because of my weight or eating habits.
18. I tend to be depressed and irritable.
19. I feel guilty when I eat.
20. I avoid some people because they bug me about the way I eat.
21. When I eat, I feel bloated and fat.
22. My eating habits and fear of food interfere with friendships or romantic relationships.
23. I binge eat.
24. I do strange things with my food (cut it into tiny pieces, eat it in special ways, eat it on special dishes with special utensils, make patterns on my plate with it, secretly throw it away, give it to the dog, hide it, spit it out before I swallow, etc.)
25. I get anxious when people watch me eat.
26. I am hardly ever satisfied with myself.
27. I vomit or take laxatives to control my weight.
28. I want to be thinner than my friends are.
29. I have said or thought, "I would rather die than be fat."
30. I have stolen food, laxatives, or diet pills from stores or from other people.
31. I have fasted to lose weight.
32. In romantic moments, I cannot let myself go because I am worried about my fat and flab.
33. I have noticed one or more of the following: cold hands and feet, dry skin, thinning hair, fragile nails, swollen glands in my neck, dental cavities, weakness, fainting, rapid or irregular heartbeat.

The greater the number of items circled, the greater the likelihood and/or tendency toward an eating disorder.

Worksheet #2
Common Myths about Eating Disorders and Dieting

Myth 1: *Eating disorders are a choice.*
Fact: People do not choose to have eating disorders. Eating disorders are illnesses. Similar to infections, eating disorders develop over time and need the appropriate treatment in order to get rid of the symptoms.

Myth 2: *Eating disorders are about food and weight.*
Fact: Eating disorders are symptoms of underlying issues. It will be important to focus on food and weight as a part of recovery, but true recovery will also involve exploring what purpose the eating disorder served, and why it developed, as well as resolving the underlying issues in order to prevent relapse.

Myth 3: *Eating disorders are "cries for attention."*
Fact: As stated above, eating disorders are not a choice. People do not develop eating disorders as a way to seek out attention. Rather, eating disorders are coping mechanisms, though faulty in nature. For this reason, it is important to address the role the eating disorder is serving for the individual, rather than writing it off as a cry for attention.

Myth 4: *As with Myth 3, "feeling fat" is a statement that people with eating disorders express for attention.*
Fact: Those with eating disorders experience a real distortion in body image. To them, looking in a mirror is the equivalent of looking in a fun house mirror. The distortion in body image is one of the symptoms of eating disorders, not a cry for attention.

Myth 5: *Purging through vomiting, laxatives, diuretics and diet pills will help lose weight.*
Fact: Purging through the means expressed above will not result in ridding the body of the food ingested in a binge. It is assumed that at most, 50% of what is consumed in a binge will remain in the body after self-induced vomiting. As for laxatives, most of the loss is fluid loss or loss of water weight, and is temporary weight loss. It is for these reasons that many people with bulimia are average or above average weight.

Myth 6: *Adding a snack, such as a serving of cookies will result in immediate weight gain.*
Fact: In order to gain one pound, a person must consume 3,500 calories over what the body needs. In order for an adolescent girl to gain one pound from cookies, she must eat an estimated equivalent of 5,700 calories. This would be 950 60-calorie cookies!

Myth 7: *Eating disorders are illnesses that affect upper middle class white females.*
Fact: Eating disorders do not discriminate. They affect people of all sexes, races, and socioeconomic classes.

Myth 8: *Eating late at night will result in weight gain.*
Fact: Unlike what is often reported in diets (and at diet centers), late night eating is not what is responsible for weight gain. It is what or how much people choose to eat late at night that may be the culprit.

Myth 9: *Eating breakfast will make you hungry.*
Fact: People who eat breakfast foods that are low in protein and fat (e.g., bagels, toast, donuts) are more likely to feel hungry shortly after the initial feelings of satisfaction because these foods contain no (or very little) protein. In order to avoid feeling hungry shortly after breakfast, choose breakfast foods that have substantial protein and a little fat, in addition to complex carbohydrates. Foods such as yogurt, cottage cheese, eggs, and peanut butter are excellent sources of protein for breakfast. Or you can be creative and healthy by eating fish such as tuna, whitefish,

or smoked salmon at breakfast as Scandinavians and Japanese people do. Foods high in protein, along with some fat and carbohydrates, promote satiety. This means you will not become hungry as soon as people who eat breakfast foods low in protein.

Myth 10: *Cutting back on calories is a sure way to lose weight.*
Fact: Those eating fewer than 1,000 calories a day are eventually more likely to gain weight than lose weight. Too little food (i.e., fuel) signals the body to shut down all auxiliary systems in order to conserve energy. This means the body burns fewer and fewer calories. The less you eat, the less you burn. This is what we call a slowed metabolism. Successful weight loss and maintenance occurs through regular healthy eating, moderate exercise, and a healthy relationship with food.

Worksheet #3
Identifying Eating-Disordered Behaviors

Do you recognize any of these behaviors in yourself? Circle the ones that you do. Star the ones that you want to change.

unconscious eating (unaware that you are eating)	eating too quickly	skipping meals
eating too much of a certain food	eating late at night	binge eating
compulsively overeating	fasting	eating for emotional reasons
"closet" eating	eating to prevent hunger	eating when too hungry
eating in response to the clock	eating while preparing	restricting intake
eating in rooms other than the kitchen	meals	restricting dairy
eating more on weekends	eating on the run	restricting protein
eating to fall asleep at night	restricting fats	eating more when alone
restricting carbohydrates	counting calories	

other (please explain): _____

Now write down the eating behaviors that you would like to change, as well as the *reasons to change* (pros) and the *reasons not to change* these behaviors (cons). Here is an example.

Behavior: *"closet" eating*

<u>Pros</u>

1. I can hide what I eat from my husband.
2. I don't feel so ashamed of my eating.

3. I can keep my anger and irritation at the kids under control when I eat anything I want.

<u>Cons</u>

1. I am gaining weight at a rapid pace.
2. I don't know how to explain why all the food is missing.
3. I want to learn to deal with my children without bingeing in secret.

Behavior: _____

<u>Pros</u>   <u>Cons</u>

_____   _____
_____   _____
_____   _____
_____   _____
_____   _____

Behavior: _____

<u>Pros</u>   <u>Cons</u>

_____   _____
_____   _____
_____   _____
_____   _____

Behavior: _____

<table>
<tr><td><u>Pros</u></td><td><u>Cons</u></td></tr>
</table>

Behavior: _____

<table>
<tr><td><u>Pros</u></td><td><u>Cons</u></td></tr>
</table>

Worksheet # 4
Understanding and Identifying Hunger

Understanding and identifying your hunger can help you learn to feed your body what and how much it needs. In order to help you understand your "hungers," we recommend that you review the following chart every time you eat.

Physical hunger: If you think hard enough, you should be able to recall times you were physically hungry. When we are physically hungry, our body lets us know. Some people get lightheaded and shaky; others have stomachs that growl or cry out for food. Regardless of what your body does, if you do not feed it enough, it is going to let you know.

Emotional hunger: This is when we eat to deal with feelings such as sadness, anger, boredom, and loneliness. When we eat for emotional reasons we do so to fill an emotional void, "stuff-down" uncomfortable or unwanted feelings, choke our anger, or punish ourselves for our neediness or negative feelings.

Social hunger: This is when we eat because food is "there" and those around us are eating. We eat to share in the ambience of the occasion, to honor the host or hostess, or to share in a celebration, such as at a birthday party. We neither over eat nor refuse to eat on such occasions.

Part I: Record hunger . . .

Hunger (P, E, S)	How hungry were you (1 – 10)	What did you eat (M, S, B)	How did you feel (SF, FL, OF)	Purge (Y/N)

Key: P = physical, E = emotional, S = social; 1–10 = least to most; M = meal; S = snack; B = Binge; SF = satisfied; FL = full; OF = over-full; Y = yes; N = no

Part II: If you noticed a tendency toward emotional eating, list the feelings you found yourself trying to stuff down or satisfy with food. Circle all that apply.

anger	anxiety	boredom	confusion	disappointment
disgust	rage	exhaustion	fear	frustration
grief	guilt	horror	hurt	jealousy
loneliness	misery	negativity	self-loathing	paranoia
puzzlement	regret	sadness	shame	

other: (explain) _____

Worksheet #5
Reaching for Your Goals

How do you cope with food? Do you cope by avoiding food?
Write how you cope by eating or not eating food. Then write more-adaptive ways to cope.

Example: I open the cabinets and stuff my face with cookies, crackers, or anything else I can get my hands on when I am seething with rage and want to hit my kids.

More-adaptive ways of coping are: Take a time-out, leave the room, go outside for some fresh air, say prayers

Now you try!

I cope by:

1) _____
2) _____
3) _____
4) _____
5) _____
6) _____

More-adaptive ways of coping are:

1) _____
2) _____
3) _____
4) _____
5) _____
6) _____
7) _____

On the following page, you will find strategies to help with your recovery. Good luck!

Recommendations for Restrictive Eating

1) Eat with someone to help challenge yourself, while minimizing the focus on food. Listen to soft music during mealtime/snack time.
2) Measure foods to make sure you aren't skimping on the serving size.
3) Plan meals/snacks ahead of time.
4) Plan to do something after the meal/snack to help with any feelings that may surface.
5) Write in journal after meals/snacks.
6) Practice allowing the "healthy voice" to have the last word over the "eating disorder voice."

Recommendations for Controlling Overeating and Binge Eating

1) Arrange to eat in one room only.
2) Do not eat while watching TV, reading, or engaging in emotional discussions.
3) Purchase individual serving-size snacks instead of regular or family-sized bags.
4) Do not "diet" . . . diets are a set up for failure. Instead work on "legalizing" food; this means incorporating "risk" foods into your meal plan on a regular (scheduled if necessary) basis.
5) Do not skip meals.
6) Sit down when eating, and focus on the food you are eating. Enjoy the texture and the flavor of the food. Take your time while eating; placing your utensils down between bites can be helpful.
7) Do not allow yourself to get too hungry before eating. Allow yourself snacks between meals as a way to prevent overeating.
8) The meal should have offerings from protein, grains, dairy, vegetable, and fruit groups, and should consist of adequate caloric intake.
9) Normalized eating, not dieting, is the first rule of recovery for all including those who are significantly overweight.
10) Meals should be spaced appropriately. Spacing may have to be rigidly tied to specific times during the day to reduce the tendency to delay eating or to overeat at certain times of the day.
11) Rigid spacing meets the goal of reducing hunger, but also it takes advantage of diet-induced thermogenesis. Frequent "stoking of the furnace" with fuel burns more calories. Consuming the same number of calories in fewer meals appears to lead to a greater accumulation of body fat. For example, rats fed twice a day versus those allowed to "nibble" freely throughout the day (fed the same number of calories per day but in the form of two large meals twice a day vs. throughout the day) gained as much as three times as much as body fat as those allowed to "nibble."

Worksheet # 6
Risk Preparation

It is important to strategize before introducing risk foods. The following two pages will help you in this endeavor.

How Safe Are Your Foods?

Please list those foods that are safe, potential, and risk foods in the columns below. The column marked N/A is for those foods that are not palatable to you.

Safe foods	Potential foods	Risk foods	N/A
_____	_____	_____	_____
_____	_____	_____	_____
_____	_____	_____	_____
_____	_____	_____	_____
_____	_____	_____	_____
_____	_____	_____	_____
_____	_____	_____	_____
_____	_____	_____	_____
_____	_____	_____	_____
_____	_____	_____	_____
_____	_____	_____	_____
_____	_____	_____	_____
_____	_____	_____	_____
_____	_____	_____	_____
_____	_____	_____	_____

Risk-Food Preparation

Step I:

Risk food I am going to introduce: _____

Where I am going to introduce this risk food: _____

Who I am going to be with when I introduce this risk food: _____

What I am going to do after I have introduced this risk food: _____

Step II:

How I feel before introducing this risk food?_____

What I am thinking before introducing this risk food? _____

_____

Do I need to challenge this thinking before introducing this risk food? _____

If so, please "challenge": _____

What am I feeling as I introduce this risk food? _____

What am I thinking as I introduce this risk food? _____

_____

Do I need to challenge this thinking? _____

If so, please "challenge": _____

_____

What am I feeling after introducing this risk food? _____

What am I thinking after introducing this risk food? _____

_____

Do I need to challenge this thinking? _____

If so, please "challenge": _____

_____

Medical Care

The PCC or primary care clinician for any patient could be an M.D., medical doctor; RNP, registered nurse practitioner; or a PA, physician's assistant. In general, any of these medical professionals can be in charge of a patient's care. However, when medication must be prescribed, a physician or medical doctor generally oversees this function.

This chapter is recommended for and directed to all medical professionals who work with patients with eating disorders, and so we will speak directly to the medical provider in our narrative. As well, non-medical professionals working with patients with eating disorders could benefit from reading this chapter to better understand the PCC's role in caring for your patients. There is a glossary explaining medical terms at the end of this chapter to facilitate your understanding of the PCC's role and the medical issues facing your patients.

Although we use the term "client" rather than "patient" in this book, in the more medically-oriented chapters—Chapters 12 and 13—we will use the term "patient," as this term more accurately reflects terminology used by the medical profession.

INTRODUCTION AND OVERVIEW

Individuals presenting with eating disorders are a challenge to treatment providers; they are as complicated as the illness itself. Each struggle is unique, with the issues often ultimately metaphors for the true struggles; the impact is devastating and sometimes deadly. An estimated 10% of patients with eating disorders will eventually die from complications. Productive and successful treatment acknowledges the complexity of eating disorders, as well as the personal suffering of the individual with the eating disorder. Empathizing with the complex struggles underlying eating disorders, the fear of the changes necessary for recovery, and the often unapparent purpose the eating disorder serves can give you a greater understanding of the demon within. Negative views of the individual as "manipulative" and "controlling" cannot facilitate a healthy patient/doctor relationship. Members of the treatment team practice patience and compassion with consequences, create clear, firm (but not rigid) contracts and boundaries and are acutely skilled listeners. Professionals cannot force the individual along the road to recovery, but they can describe that road, make it as smooth, straight, and minimally bumpy as possible and accompany the patient along it. The more bumps and turns the team creates, the more resistant to change the individual and family are likely to become.

Therefore, the goal for the treatment team is to develop and implement a clear, comprehensive treatment plan which evolves as the patient and her illness change. Struggles between the patient and the treatment must be dealt with clearly, compassionately, and consistently; inconsistencies between the different members of the team will provoke the patient's maladaptive coping techniques. Clear guidelines and boundaries at the beginning of and throughout treatment can best diffuse some future treatment struggles. The best treatment approach combines a multidimensional team of professionals focusing on the medical, nutritional, and psychological consequences of the eating disorder. This team includes any combination of primary care clinician (hereafter PCC, which can be physician, Nurse Practitioner or Physician's Assistant), individual therapist, nutritionist, psychopharmacologist (possibly the PCC), family therapist, and group therapist. At times other clinicians (such as a gynecologist), or a sports coach or a school representative may be team members. On these teams, "too many cooks *do not* spoil the soup" as long as the patient and each member of the team has been involved in creating the recipe (the contract) and is clear and consistent in his/her participation in the cooking (the treatment plan). Defining each professional's role helps both the individual team members and the client understand how the team functions. Whenever possible, the individual should also be included as a part of the team; this inclusion can provide a sense of empowerment for the individual, and prevent certain struggles and resistance in treatment.

USUAL DIVISION OF ROLES

The PCC's focus is on medical well-being. The PCC:

1. Helps with the diagnosis by excluding alternative etiologies for the symptoms.
2. Establishes the weight goal (short and long term) and rate for weight gain.
3. Determines what constitutes medical health for the individual.
4. Provides medical monitoring and assesses medical safety.
5. Makes nutritional and exercise recommendations.
6. Makes recommendations for hospitalization based on medical criteria.

The nutritionist works with the patient to determine a meal plan based on the physician's recommendations for weight goals and medical health, while assisting the patient in articulating and addressing her fears of food, weight, and body image.

The primary therapist or mental health professional:

1. Serves as the case manager and coordinator of the patient's care.
2. Helps the patient understand the purpose and meaning of the eating disorder for her.
3. Works with the patient to explore the feelings associated with the team's goals and nutritional recommendations.
4. Explores cognitive and behavioral strategies to create change to foster recovery.
5. Makes recommendations for hospitalization based on psychiatric criteria.

The psychopharmacologist, who is typically a psychiatrist, but may be the PCC, works with the patient to provide medication management when necessary in order to facilitate the treatment goals.

OFFICE PREPARATION FOR THE PRIMARY CARE CLINICIAN

Even before a patient has entered your office, review the following:

The Waiting Room: Understanding eating disorders means acknowledging the impact the media and culture have on society. Remove items in your waiting room that reinforce the negative messages that contribute to the development of eating disorders, such as emphasis on weight, appearance, and diets. Have literature which emphasizes wellness. Consider eliminating literature presenting "how to look" or that shows unrealistic body images. You'll be surprised at how many popular magazines you may eliminate for this reason. In doing so, you are sending healthier messages to *all* your patients.

Staff and Chart: Have a notation on the chart (perhaps on the problem list) queuing the staff that this patient has an eating disorder. Teach staff *not* to discuss weight and appearance as they chat with these patients. Also note specifics of patient care including *how and where* the patient is to be weighed, whether the patient may be told her weight, and the frequency of urine testing (see below).

Scale: Be sure that there is a scale in a private area or one that can be moved into one. This avoids the patient's feeling "exposed" or "gawked at." One of the paradoxes of this disease is the simultaneous satisfaction and shame the patient feels about her body.

INITIAL VISIT WITH THE PRIMARY CARE CLINICIAN FOR A PATIENT KNOWN TO HAVE AN EATING DISORDER

As part of the initial evaluation, do not have the staff weigh the patient before she is seen. The patient should be allowed to remain dressed in street clothes (not in a johnny) for the initial interview. The patient will be very self-conscious, and being clothed will allow her to focus more on your discussion and less on her body in a johnny. As you interview her, listen for issues of shaming, trust, guilt, distortion. Listen for issues of control, such as someone "made" her eat or something happened and she had to vomit. Eventually, your goal is to talk with her about which choices she can make which allow her to feel, and be, healthy. Near the end of the visit, have the patient change into a johnny so you can weigh, and examine her and take her vitals. She will have had the opportunity to feel heard by you. She will know you are interested in her well-being. Her weight will be only one of many factors you will consider as you fashion a care plan for her.

Within your usual history, specifically focus on the following areas:

1. Weight history—under-/overweight in elementary and high school, weight at graduations, marriage, etc.
2. Nutrition overview—ask about food choices, exclusions, and patterns of eating. Notice whether your client is unconcerned or pleased about low weight, any bingeing or purging. Be specific in your line of questioning—how many cookies (or boxes of cookies) constitute a binge, etc. Nutritionist will be more thorough.
3. Exercise—note amount and frequency. Listen for healthy exercise pattern versus obsession.
4. Gynecological issues—find out your client's onset of menses, regularity now and in the past, and amenorrhea. Clarify sexual activity, number and sex(es) of partner(s), contraception, risks for sexually transmitted diseases (and any prior testing), number of pregnancies, abortions, miscarriages, or still births. Review any history of and treatment for infertility.
5. Ask about any physical, emotional, or sexual trauma or abuse.
6. Gastrointestinal symptoms, as specific reflections of nutritional issues, vomiting, or laxative use, and more general ones such as abdominal pain, bloating, and constipation.
7. Symptoms of dehydration
8. Heat or cold intolerance.
9. Notice whether there is a long list of unexplained or vague symptoms. These may follow a pattern which can lead you to another new diagnosis, or may be somatization of emotions.

10. Ask about any use of herbs, teas, or any non-prescription treatments or treatments by other clinicians.

11. In the family history, look for addictions (including workaholism and gambling in addition to substances), mental illness (including obsessive-compulsive disorder, bipolar illness, otherwise known as manic-depression), anxiety, and eating disorders, which may not have been specifically diagnosed or are not discussed within the family). Review weight history within the family tree. The manner in which these questions are answered or evaded may be as diagnostic as the actual information.

MAKING AN INITIAL DIAGNOSIS OF AN EATING DISORDER

In all routine exams, keep the eating disorder diagnosis in mind. Numerous studies have found that the incidence of anorexia nervosa occurs in 1% of all young women, and the incidence of bulimia in 20% of young women. Both diseases occur less frequently in men. In making your intitial diagnosis, review the 11 history questions noted above. Consider an eating disorder diagnosis especially when weight and appearance are important factors in the success of those who choose certain occupations or activities, such as with wrestlers, dancers, cheerleaders, and models. Think of the eating disorder diagnoses when there is a family or personal history of addictions, if a patient has unusual difficulty with the pelvic exam or if there is a fracture with minimal trauma (suggestive of osteoporosis). Consider these eating disorder diagnoses when there is a long list of unexplained, vague somatic complaints, amenorrhea, symptoms of dehydration, or symptoms which are potentially the consequences of vomiting, laxatives, or excessive exercise.

Physical Exam

During your usual exam, focus on the following assessments:

1. Vital Signs
   - Height
   - Weight (note whether in clothes or johnny)
   - Temperature
   - Supine blood pressure (BP) and Heart Rate (HR)
   - Standing BP and HR
2. Overall appearance, increase or decrease of muscle mass, and/or body fat
3. Skin
   - pale, sallow/yellowish
   - lanugo (fine hair on face, arms)
   - axillary and pubic hair present
   - scars on dorsum of hands from self-induced vomiting
4. Adenopathy
5. Is there any parotid gland enlargement?
6. Are enamel of teeth damaged?
7. Although a routine gynecological exam is usually a part of an initial assessment, you may defer this to follow-up, to minimize the sense of vulnerability of the patient.

In making the diagnosis, symptoms of anorexia nervosa include: restrictive eating, menstrual irregularities (especially amenorrhea), cold intolerance, constipation, excessive weight loss (often after an intentional small weight loss), and being underweight and either feeling unconcerned or pleased about this. Signs of anorexia nervosa include hypotension and bradycardia, hypothermia, lanugo, muscle atrophy, carotenemia, arrhythmias, hair loss, elevated LFTs without symptoms, mild anemia (not due to iron or folate deficiency) and bone density loss.

Signs and symptoms of bulimia are often minimal, absent or not revealed by the patient; the patient generally looks fine.

Specific symptoms of bulimia include: vomiting, chest pain (from GE reflux), the feeling that she has to get food out of her body, and polyuria (from fluid loading). Some of these patients also exhibit other high-risk behavior relating to addictions, STDs, or reckless sports. Signs of bulimia include: wide weight fluctuations, parotid gland enlargement, scars on fingers (from vomiting), loss of tooth enamel, electrolyte abnormalities, and blood sugars too low or too high.

Symptoms common to anorexia nervosa and bulimia include: nutritional deficiencies, binge eating, over-exercising, muscle cramps and spasms, lightheadedness, abdominal pain, constipation, "bloating"(when others see a flat abdomen), depression, anxiety, irritability, fatigue, difficulty sleeping, isolation from friends and/or family, preoccupation with food, preoccupation with weight, "feeling fat," having "good" and "bad" foods, food rituals, making excuses not to eat, feeling relieved when not eating, and difficulty and/or refusal to eat foods from any particular food group. "Does food control your life?" may be a helpful screening question. Signs of both anorexia and bulimia include: low glucose levels, orthostatic changes in vital signs, weight loss.

Initial Assessment and Plan

At the conclusion of the first visit, a preliminary assessment is made based on the history, physical, and assessment of stage of change. This may be modified based on the labs and discussion among treatment team members. The recommendations and plan will be determined by the following:

If you are uncertain of the diagnosis, order labs necessary for the differential diagnosis of symptoms (such as weight loss, change in menstrual history, change in body hair, etc.) and schedule a follow-up (a long appointment with enough time for the necessary discussion) as soon as you anticipate that the labs will return, to discuss the diagnosis and treatment. This discussion *must* occur in person. A phone call from you or a staff member to discuss the initial diagnosis and plan for an eating disorder is not adequate.

If you confirm an eating disorder diagnosis:

1. Order labs that are needed to assess the state of this disease.
2. Advise the patient at what stage of preparation for change you see her (see below).
3. Discuss the treatment team. Clarify that, in order to care for her, she must authorize all members of the treatment team to share information freely. This is rarely a problem. If she initially refuses, refer this to the individual therapist. Ultimately, it is almost impossible to adequately treat a patient who will not allow all of her treatment team to have free discussion.
4. Explain the PCC role, including initial frequency of office visits and labs and what future office visits will routinely involve. Begin to negotiate how vital signs will be done, and why. Educate the patient about risks of malnutrition, amenorrhea, chronic vomiting, laxatives, diuretics, diet pills, ipecac use, and osteoporosis with amenorrhea. Discuss the fallacy that diuretics and laxatives promote weight loss, and the risks of cardiac and proximal muscle myopathy with ipecac use (see below)
5. Ask her for any questions, arrange lab testing and next appointment.
6. Any other treating clinicians should be informed (such as gynecologists), so that one comprehensive diagnostic and treatment plan is created.

7. Consult other team members to create the initial treatment plan. Don't feel isolated or overwhelmed; you are a member of a team that will together create and revise this patient's treatment plan.

Laboratory Evaluation

Tests commonly ordered to assess eating disorders include CBC (complete blood count), electrolytes, BUN (blood urea nitrogen), creatinine, glucose, liver function, TSH (thyroid-stimulating hormone), serum HCG (human chorionic gonadotropin), amylase, albumin, calcium, magnesium, and rarely, pituitary function evaluations. This list is a partial list; it is not meant to imply that all these tests should be ordered routinely, or that others are inappropriate.

What you're looking for in these labs in relation to eating disorders is:

CBC: Anorexia commonly causes anemia, leukopenia or both. Have a baseline. A patient whose baseline WBC is 2.8, then suddenly elevates to 6.0 has a relative leukocytosis. A gradual elevation is more likely an improvement in the disease state. Unless the absolute neutropil count is under 1000, these patients do not seem clinically to be immunodefficient. Anemia can be due to malnutrition itself, but specific nutritional deficiencies should be evaluated.

Glucose: hypo- or hyper-glycemia, if present, are important factors in assessing the severity of the eating disorder. Episodes of hypo- and hyper-glycemia may be seen with bulimia, depending on the restrictive or bingeing phase of the illness relative to the blood drawing.

Liver function tests may become asymptomatically elevated with severe anorexia nervosa. This is due to distorted physiology of severe malnutrition.

Amylase: with a history of vomiting and in the absence of abdominal pain, differentiating between salivary versus pancreatic origin of an elevated amylase is unnecessary.

Thyroid function: to evaluate weight status and gynecological issues, a TSH is an adequate screen in most cases.

Serum HCG, prolactin: (only if presence of galactorrhea) to evaluate irregular menses/amenorrhea. (Depending on your expertise, if significant gynecological issues are present, you may evaluate them or refer to a gynecologist who is sensitive to working with a patient with an eating disorder.)

EKG: administer EKG as a baseline in those at risk for severe malnutrition or electrolyte abnormalities

Calcium, magnesium for a patient at risk for arrhythmias due to electrolyte imbalance from severe vomiting and/or diuretic use.

Cholesterol: exercise caution here—there is little reason to order cholesterol testing, and it can be elevated in anorexia nervosa. *Do not* recommend a low fat diet for an elevated cholesterol to a person who is *significantly* underweight. If the cholesterol is elevated, it is a reflection of the distorted metabolism of malnutrition, not an indication of increased risk for heart disease.

Albumin: administer this test only for a baseline with prolonged, severe malnutrition. A normal value is of no value, but a low one should be evaluated for other causes (GI or renal losses) and if attributed to the anorexia, is very worrisome.

Additional tests of adrenals, pituitary, GI, only if specifically indicated.

Bone density to assess for osteoporosis—consider initially only with prolonged, severe malnutrition or with a history of fractures with minor trauma.

Urinanylasis—to monitor specific gravity and the presence or absence of ketones (suggesting severe malnutrition with a ketotic state).

MEDICAL GUIDELINES FOR OUTPATIENT MANAGEMENT

In all cases, the goals of treatment are normal weight, and a healthy relationship with food and exercise.

1. *Weight goal.* Normal weight is a BMI of 21 in females and 22 in males. A reasonable weight goal for treatment is either the weight at which this patient previously menstruated (usually 85–90% of normal weight) or 90% of a normal BMI.
2. *Goal for rate of weight gain.* A reasonable goal for weight gain is 2–3 pounds per month (which is an average of .5–1 pounds per week). Many patients who are gaining or losing weight do so in steps rather than perfectly linearly, so this monthly overview demonstrates the true trends without struggling about half-pound variations at each visit. Faster weight gain risks edema, CHF, and bulimia, and should be evaluated.
3. *Exercise* is encouraged or restricted based on the medical stability of the patient. Exercise may represent many things for these patients, from a way to burn "bad food" calories, to a physical means to suppress and thus manage feelings, to a ritual behavior. Many of these patients may be accomplished athletes, for whom the potential loss of team membership or status is unacceptable. Exercise is initially rarely geared toward enjoyment and wellness. A major function of the PCC is making exercise prescriptions which, while sensitive to the above issues, permit medical amelioration for the patient. The support of therapist, coaches, and family members is critical. Initial lack of support from family and community may reveal important contributions to the patient's illness and demonstrate systemic problems, which need to change for the patient to become well. Team support for the PCC, who sometimes feels in the middle of this conflict, is invaluable.

PROCHASKA'S STAGES OF CHANGE THEORY FOR THE MEDICAL PROVIDER

The best treatment plan is individually tailored to the patient's needs and clearly defines the roles and boundaries of each team member. Prochaska's Stages of Change theory (reviewed in the introduction and throughout the book) provides a valuable conceptual framework for creating and revising the treatment plan. This is illustrated below, in recommendations for each stage. Again, these are guidelines and will not be appropriate for all patients at any given stage.

Stage 1: Precontemplation

The patient presenting in the stage of Precontemplation is either in denial or unaware that she has a problem. The PCC's role with this patient is to provide education, form an alliance, gather information from other clinicians and family members, provide medical and nutritional information, and provide general medical coverage. The patient does not have the same understanding of her struggles as you do, nor is she as motivated for recovery as you are for her. If you as the PCC have made the initial diagnosis, she may not even agree to see a nutritionist or therapist because "there's nothing wrong with me." At this stage, alliance and education are key. Motivation for recovery is not an issue to be addressed in this stage; it will be explored as the patient moves on in her stages to recovery.

Regardless of the patient's acceptance of the diagnosis, medical safety and stability must be assessed. In general, patients presenting in Precontemplation benefit from a treatment contract which outlines what the patient needs to maintain medical safety and avoid a more intensive treatment approach. The contract should focus on medical issues, such as weight, vital signs, and keeping appointments than on behavioral issues (which are treatment foci in later stages). Balancing accuracy with sensitivity to the patient, you will routinely need: 1) a urine sample *before* each weight (to minimize weight fluctuations from a full bladder) and 2) to weigh the patient in a johnny. As denial at this stage is strong, these measures maximize accuracy and respectfully challenge the denial, while acknowledging tampering (such as fluid loading). We strongly recommend that you do not inform your patient of her actual weight, but rather whether she has lost, maintained, or gained; at this stage the patient is not ready to use these numbers constructively, despite her stated desire to know her weight.

Stage 2: Contemplation

In the stage of Contemplation, the patient is aware of her problem, but her fear of change limits her ability to envision or implement effective action. As with the stage of Precontemplation, the patient in Contemplation may not be as ready for recovery as you are for her. Your role as educator continues, with you now also being the recipient of information/education from the patient. At this stage, the patient is afraid to give up these symptoms which are (sometimes unconsciously) serving a purpose for her. It is important for you to accept (without necessarily understanding nor approving) that the eating disorder is in some way helping her, despite its negative consequences. As your alliance with her develops, you (and the therapist) will discuss various treatment options and/or plans, which could serve the same function with less detrimental effects. The goal is to help the patient challenge her ambivalence and prepare to make change (which constitutes the stage of Preparation). With the worksheet "The Struggle with Change" you can help your patient explore the disadvantages and detriments of her eating disorder, especially if she is not yet agreeing to see a therapist. This information should be saved, as it will be an invaluable part of recovery.

From the medical standpoint, you may be more flexible in your exam of the patient at this stage. You are no longer challenging denial, but helping the patient gather and accept the information, which will ultimately lead her to accept that change is critical. As she is likely more reliable with data, you may alter the protocol in ways that demonstrate you respect her honesty. Instead of being weighed in a johnny, you may offer her the option of being weighed in a T-shirt and shorts. Alternatively, you may recommend less frequent visits or labs. You and she may discuss whether she would benefit from, or become more anxious about knowing, her exact weight at each visit. Although initially eager to know her weight, she may not yet be able to use the information to implement healthy change. At this stage, there is now open discussion and negotiation as you together sit with her ambiguity and fear of change.

Stage 3: Preparation

In the stage of Preparation, the goal is to help the patient develop a strategy for making a plan toward change. Education and acceptance of the fears associated with change continue to be important. The PCC's role is to help the patient develop an initial plan for symptom reduction, define how success and failure will be measured and monitored, and develop a "back up" plan around medical and weight issues. Whenever possible, remind her of the consequences (both positive and negative) of her actions, and remind her that her treatment team and other significant people in her life will help to facilitate her initial attempts to implement change. Most of the cognitive and behavioral issues in the stage of Preparation take place in the therapist's office. Certain circumstances, however, are more medically based and should take place between you and the patient. For example, the PCC and the patient determine decisions regarding weight and exercise. A patient who is trying to increase her weight must evaluate the relative possibility, for her, of increasing food intake or decreasing exercise. If the patient is not yet learning her actual weight at each visit, you should explore during this stage whether she is yet able to use this data beneficially. In most cases, working with numbers on the scale has been more beneficial than detrimental. The worksheet, "Getting Ready for Behavioral Change," provides guided questions for your discussion and mutual treatment planning in the stage of Preparation.

Stage 4: Action

The patient presenting in the stage of Action has identified her eating disorder, is aware of her fears associated with recovery, understands the harmfulness of the disorder, and has begun to enact a plan for recovery. This is the stage of practice. It is important to understand that the strategies developed in this stage represent uncharted territories. The patient feels an increased readiness to explore these grounds, but this will be difficult. Your support and encouragement of each effort (regardless of the outcome) provide strength for her to attempt additional new strategies to cope with feelings, urges, and pressures that arise. While you are not the therapist, the value of your alliance with the patient at this stage is significant. The greater your empathy, the more you can honestly acknowledge the courage she is exhibiting in her attempts, the more effectively you and she can negotiate the medical and physical details which are ever present at this stage, and the stronger is your alliance with her. Those strategies that appear more psychologically based should be deferred to her next appointment with her therapist. As with any major life change, relapses will be part of the journey, and these must be used as opportunities for learning. Avoid showing disappointment or overlooking the opportunity to review the experience and derive alternative options.

Stage 5: Maintenance

When change has been taking place for six months, with an expressed increase in ease, the patient can be considered to be in the stage of Maintenance. During this stage, the focus should be on prevention of relapse as well as the reinforcement of current coping skills and change. The patient in this stage is attempting to solidify a lifestyle change, and is feeling increased ease in her new behaviors. Discussion can now be broadened to include expanded ways to improve self-care. At this point, decrease the frequency of visits and the focus on the eating disorder, food, and weight. The new goal is to help the patient explore her new identity, and help her let go of her eating-disordered identity. This is the final stage before the stage of mastery.

Stage 6: Termination

This stage never really happens with the PCC, because such providers continue to manage ongoing wellness, preventive care, and illnesses with the patient. Only for administrative or geographical reasons does the PCC terminate, not at a stage of treatment. It is incredibly rewarding to follow a patient with whom one has worked through these struggles, and who now has a healthy relationship with food and balance in her life, and can go on to other issues. However, under major life stresses, traces of the eating disorder may emerge. It is critical to be sensitive to this possibility.

The patient needs to know her PCC will always be available to her, including in health. She needs to know she may call the PCC with questions and concerns and, despite her newfound health, she must never fail to see the PCC for regular check-ups and preventative care.

GUIDELINES FOR HOSPITALIZATION AND FOLLOW-UP

Medical Guidelines for Hospitalization

1. Weight loss of 40% below ideal or below premorbid weight (or 30% if loss within 3 months). A BMI of 15 defines medically significant starvation.
2. Potentially serious cardiac arrhythmias, including tachyarrythmias and bradycardia.
3. Persistent hypokalemia or hyponatremia, which is not quickly (24 hours), corrected with out-patient treatment.
4. Symptoms of inadequate cerebral perfusion (dizziness, syncope).
5. Unstable vital signs, either hypothermia or postural hypotension (especially without compensatory tachycardia).

Psychiatric Guidelines for Hospitalization

1. Serious suicidal ideation with inability to contract for safety.
2. Severe depression.
3. Rarely, with severe and persistent malnutrition, there may be loss of judgment, insight, and mental clarity, which are judged as incompetence to make treatment decisions. Clearly, psychiatry and the legal system are involved at this stage.

Follow-up Visits

Before the patient and PCC meet, the staff should collect data on the patient's weight, postural vital signs, and (in some cases) test urine for ketones and specific gravity. Be sure the staff checks the charts before the patient is seen to learn which data must be collected, in which manner, and whether the patient is to know the data. Have staff report to you any questionable information or suspicious behavior, and be very sensitive to your patient's potential embarrassment and shame about the visit.

1. *Weight:* Depending on the severity of malnutrition, the presence of deceptive behavior, the stage of change (and thus the value to the patient of knowing the data) you make decisions regarding ways to weigh patients along a spectrum from least to most potentially humiliating and accurate. Some clinicians start all patients with the most accurate methods, and let her "earn" being weighed in street clothes. This involves the patient wearing only a johnny to be weighed. Alternatively, unless the patient is medically unstable, you may minimize the patient's discomfort by weighing her in street clothes, with empty pockets and shoes off, or in shorts and a T-shirt. See discussion of stages of change, above, as a guideline. If the team has contracted that the weight not be discussed on each visit, the patient should be weighed with her back to the scale.
2. *Vital signs:* Postural vital signs including blood pressure (BP) and pulse (P), and temp must be taken on each visit. Routine: Patient's weight is taken and she is instructed to lie down on the exam table. Patient is *left lying down* for *at least* 3 minutes (staff does other work) then BP and P are taken *lying down*. Patient then stands, and BP and P are repeated. Staff should note any symptoms in the patient during this time. The patient then lies or sits down to wait for you. As these patients are thin and often cold, staff can offer a blanket or extra Johnny to wear while the patient is waiting to see you.

3. *Urine sample:* Urine should be tested periodically on stable or improving patients, but at every visit on patients who are very malnourished, regularly vomiting and/or fluid overloading, and on patients in early stages of change, to assess specific gravity and ketones. Only with the rare, highly deceptive patient must the collection of the urine be supervised or at least the sample container inconspicuously labeled so that you are certain that the sample tested was just produced by the patient. This should be analyzed by the staff (not sent off to the lab) so that the data is available to you when you see the patient.

Continuing Care

Whenever you see the patient in your office, ask how *she* thinks that she is doing. This tells you her insight. Ask how well she has been able to comply with the plan from the last visit. When appropriate, ask specific questions about vomiting, laxatives, and diuretics. You are looking for data, not value judgments (e.g., "I ate 2 meals a day" vs. "I'm doing well"). Periodically monitor for other at-risk behavior regarding risk-taking with automobiles and sports, drugs, alcohol or unsafe sex. Monitor exercise and relaxation. Ask about herbs, teas, or any non-prescription treatments or treatments by other clinicians.

If the patient gives you much information that is to be dealt with by the therapist, unless it is life threatening, redirect her to share that with the therapist. Giving the wrong information to the wrong team member is one of the ways the therapeutic work may be undermined (e.g., a patient tells the physician her feelings and denies any physical symptoms then tells the therapist about her dizziness and headaches and minimizes emotions). If it occurs, the team must constantly reeducate the patient about giving the correct information to the correct team member, and the therapist may explore whether this behavior pattern is reproduced elsewhere in the patient's life.

As you interview her, be sensitive to underlying issues of shaming, trust, guilt, or distortion. Listen for issues of control (which you can reframe as choices for health/wellness). As you are her PCC, ask if there are any issues other than the eating disorder that she wishes to discuss. A physical exam relevant to the state of the patient's disease and any other medical issues is done. For patients who are seen once a week or more, the vital signs may be enough.

Lastly, review the information and state your assessment as of this visit. Be specific about your assessment of her stage of change, progress, or regression (noting or withholding specific data as per the contract) and make recommendations for this visit. Early on, the patient is likely to be passive, but in the later stages there may be healthy negotiations with her about what seems possible to her, and what seems necessary to you, for her to make medical progress. When there is major crisis with the work with the therapist, knowing this (from the therapist) before the patient visits may lead you to support her for maintaining her state as she does difficult emotional work, whereas at another point you might urge her to make more medical change. Reeducate her often regarding cause, effect, and complications of her behaviors. Periodically reeducate her about risks and fallacies of malnutrition, amenorrhea, chronic vomiting, laxatives, diuretics, diet pills, ipecac use, and osteoporosis with amenorrhea. Consider bone density testing to evaluate for osteoporosis, or treating amenorrhea with oral contraceptive (OCP) for osteoporosis prevention. If patient is on an OCP, consider stopping it when she is near 85–90% of normal BMI, to see if menses return.

If you feel a change in the treatment is needed, advise her of this and explain how this will be communicated to other members of the team. If labs are to be done, arrange for them to be communicated along with your recommendations as soon as results are available. Clarify whether a message can be left on an answering machine or voice mail, or with a family member, or whether the patient should be directed to call for results. At the end of each session be clear and unambiguous about follow-up by you and by the patient.

A FEW OTHER ISSUES

Communication with Other Team Members

Depending on the stage of treatment and instability of the patient, communication may be periodic or after each visit. It is critical for all team members to know when a patient "no shows" an appointment or if there is a pattern of repeated cancellations of appointments. Information communicated varies by patient, but will usually include: actual weight, weight change since last visit, and any medical instability or new medical issues. Any struggles which were observed, such as between a patient and parent regarding weight or exercise, or any deception, should be communicated. This may be done by faxing the flow sheet, leaving a message on a clinician's confidential voice mail, or whatever easy and confidential system you set up among the team. Any changes in the contract must be communicated to all team members in a timely manner.

Patient Contracts

At certain points in treatment, it is very valuable to make a written contract between the patient and the treatment team. Issues to be addressed in this are:

1. Weight goals and goal for speed of weight gain (see above).
2. Whether the patient and/or family members will know the weight. Some patients find it very stressful to know the exact weight on each visit, so the team, primarily the therapist, may negotiate with the patient that she will be told either nothing, or only that she has gained or lost. If information is withheld, it is often helpful to negotiate a point at which the information will be shared—such as when there has been a 5 pound weight change, or when 90% of the goal has been reached, or such. In addition, knowledge of the weight change is a powerful issue within the family, so negotiating with the patient and family who will know the weight is critical. It is critical that the staff follow these guidelines and not accidentally tell the information to the patient or family. It is often unwise to have the family know the weight if the patient does not.
3. The consequences of further weight loss and/or medical instability from bulimic behavior. Patients often try to maintain a "normal" life and seek treatment, and this may be unsuccessful. Conditions must be clearly agreed upon *in advance*, relating to exercise, more aggressive outpatient treatment, partial hospitalization or inpatient admission. Issues to include are:
   a. exercise. Medically, if the patient cannot gain weight, energy expenditure must be limited. These women are often successful athletes who will object to this, but our focus must be, with compassion, on improved wellness. Exercise is then resumed, gradually, only when it can occur with continued nutritional and weight progress.
   b. criteria for "intensification of treatment" will include regression or failure to progress, usually negotiated by the therapist.
   c. criteria for hospitalization (see above) includes psychiatric and medical instability. A patient may receive I.V. hydration in an outpatient setting on rare occasions, but hospitalization at a psychiatric hospital which can give medical support is needed rather than a medical unit, because it is the eating disorder, not a primary medical disorder, which underlies the medical instability.

GLOSSARY OF MEDICAL TERMINOLOGY
FOR NON-MEDICALLY-TRAINED CLINICIANS

Basic Symptomotology

Temperature: Lowered body temperature reflects dehydration, lowered blood pressure, and an insufficient layer of fat.

Blood pressure (BP): Low Blood Pressure (Hypotention) reflects lowered body temperature, dehydration, and malnutrition. Tends to occur in those struggling with anorexia nervosa.

Orthostatic Hypotention refers to a sudden drop in blood pressure upon standing or sitting up.

High Blood Pressure (Hypertension) refers to blood pressure that is greater than 140 over 90. Tends to occur in those struggling with binge eating.

Heart rate: A lowered heart rate reflects malnutrition, dehydration, and a low blood pressure. All common symptoms associated with anorexia nervosa.

Weight: A measurement of one's weight helps determine medical stability and measures significant changes that can put pressure on the heart.

Larugo: A soft downy hair that appears on the face, arms, and back as a response to starvation and malnutrition. It is the body's mechanism to keep itself warm as body temperature decreases.

Edema: The swelling of joints, abdomen, and feet as a result of excess water accumulation. This is frequently found in those who purge by vomiting and/or laxatives.

Swollen face: Often referred to as "chipmunk cheeks," a swollen face is a common symptom of those who vomit frequently.

Bruised fingers: As with the swollen face, bruised fingers can be a sign of self-induced vomiting.

Bruised skin: Frequent bruising can be a result of vitamin deficiencies, extreme weight loss, and low blood pressure.

Cold hands and feet: Poor circulation can result from starvation and malnutrition.

The Blood Tests

Complete Blood Count (CBC): A CBC will check for anemia, infection, and immune-system functionality. This occurs through white blood cell count, red blood cell count, and platelets count.

Electrolytes: Needed to maintain healthy body function, electrolytes are a combination of minerals the body needs to maintain balance. An electrolyte imbalance can cause kidney failure, heart attack, and possible death.

Blood glucose (blood sugar): Hyperglycemia is a high blood sugar level, and may be seen in blood drawn within 1 hour of eating, and in bulimia. Persistent elevated levels suggest diabetes mellitus. Hypoglycemia is a low blood sugar level, and if severe can be life threatening. It is seen in bulimia and severe anorexia nervosa.

Blood urea nitrogen (BUN): The level of urea in the blood is a rough estimate of kidney function. An increase in the BUN level usually indicates decreased kidney function.

Cholesterol: Important to maintain a healthy heart, it is important to make sure the ratio of "good" (HDL; high-density lipid) to "bad" (LDL; low-density lipid) cholesterol is within normal limits. High "bad" cholesterol and low "good" cholesterol can lead to a heart attack and possible death.

B12 and folic acid: Important in the assessment of depression and anxiety, a lack of vitamin B12 and folic acid can lead to difficulties with the body's ability to absorb nutrients. This, in turn, can lead to difficulties with metabolizing protein, carbohydrates, and fat.

Thyroid function: The thyroid gland is in your neck, and is usually barely palpable. The thyroid gland controls metabolism, so an elevated level (hyperthyroidism) causes weight loss, sweating, a rapid heart beat, and irregular menses; and a low level (hypothyroidism) causes weight gain, fatigue, and irregular or absent menses. Hypothyroidism is very common in the general population. Thyroid function is measured by TSH (thyroid-stimulating hormone), which is the messenger from the pituitary gland to the thyroid. So, the value of the TSH is inverse to the thyroid dysfunction: an elevated TSH suggests an underactive thyroid (the pituitary is calling louder for more thyroid hormone production) and an abnormally low TSH suggests excess thyroid hormone (hyperthyroidism).

Liver function: Although this test is not needed often, Elevated liver enzymes can reflect liver disease, gallbladder disease, or whether the patient has had a heart attack.

Kidney function: As with the liver function test, this test is not needed often. It is performed to assess kidney function, an important test for those with eating disorders, and for patients taking certain medications.

The Urine Tests

Complete urinalysis: Helps to assess the function of the kidneys, urine sugar, and ketone levels. This also helps with diagnosis of a variety of systemic diseases and urinary tract disorders. The urinanylasis is a sample of the urine that is measured for many tests. Some test results are immediately available, such as "dipstick" tests with many chemical tests individually placed on a strip of paper that is dipped into the urine. Within 2 minutes, colors may change for indicators of various chemical reactions, indicating the presence or absence of sugar (glucose), protein, ketones, WBC (white blood cell count), RBC (red blood cell count), plus measuring the specific gravity.

Ketones: Starvation and malnutrition can cause ketones to accumulate in the blood, indicating the body is breaking down fat in the body for energy. This accumulation of ketones in the blood can cause coma or death.

Other Tests

Echocardiogram or Electrocardiogram: ECG or EKG are electrocardiograms. This is a recording of the electrical activity of the heart, done by placing 6 electrical strips at certain points on the chest and 3 on the limbs (one on each arm and one on either leg). These can be very complicated to interpret, and reflect the electrical not the mechanical function of the heart. For our purposes, they show the rate and rhythm of the heart beat, and may suggest other problems, but will not necessarily show damage to the heart by malnutrition. Other tests, such as a cardiac ultrasound, visually record the motion of the heart, and can show changes in the size and function of the heart muscle itself and the valves. These tests help with the identification of causes associated with heart irregularities.

Bone density testing: Helps identify osteoporosis (bone loss) caused by calcium and vitamin D deficiencies and/or hormonal imbalances (amenorrhea).

Infertility testing: Important for those women wishing to conceive who are having difficulty getting pregnant. Eating disorders can lead to high-risk pregnancy, problems with fetal development, and birth defects.

Other Terms

Amylase is a digestive hormone secreted by the salivary glands and the pancreas. It is elevated with pancreatitis and also with vomiting, so it is commonly elevated with bulimia.

Prolactin is a hormone secreted by the pituitary gland, related to milk production by the breast. It can also be secreted by a tumor of the pituitary. An elevated prolactin causes irregular or absent menses, especially indicated by a milky discharge from the breast, so a test for prolactin levels may be ordered to evaluate menstrual irregularities.

Calcium and magnesium are minerals which are regulated by complex mechanisms in the body. Calcium and magnesium supplements do not directly relate to these blood levels and questions related to these should be directed to the PCC.

Albumin is a protein made by the liver, and a low level can reflect severe malnutrition.

SUMMARY

In conclusion, the actual medical management of a patient with an eating disorder is straightforward. What makes caring for these patients challenging is the constant personal surveillence that the clinician must keep, so we do not casually slip and talk about body size, or say "just eat." These issues are metaphors for *very difficult* underlying struggles for each patient, and the language we use can convey either compassion and concern, or criticism and disbelief.

The following pages contain an Initial Assessment form for the Primary Care Clinician, and valuable worksheets that can be given to the patient.

THE INITIAL ASSESSMENT

Patient Name: _____ D.O.B. _____

Address:_____ Insurance: _____

_____

Phone: (H) _____

(W)_____

Emergency Contact: _____ Relation: _____

Phone: _____

Reason for visit (in patient's words): _____

_____

_____

Personal history:

   Does patient live alone or with someone? _____

      (If patient lives with someone, whom does she live with? _____

   Does patient live in a home, apartment, dorm, specialty housing? _____

   Does patient work? _____ If "yes," what does she do? _____

   What is patient's level of education? _____

   Is patient here at her own will, or at the advice of someone else? _____

Family History:

   Mother's Name: _____ Age: _____

   Occupation: _____

   Father's Name: _____ Age: _____

   Occupation: _____

   Siblings' Names (if applicable):

   Sister(s): _____ Age: _____

   _____ _____

   _____ _____

   _____ _____

   _____ _____

   Brother(s): _____ Age: _____

   _____ _____

   _____ _____

   _____ _____

   _____ _____

(genogram)

Is there a family history of any of the following (If "yes" please list the family relationship):

High blood pressure: _____ _____

Heart disease: _____ _____

High cholesterol: _____ _____

Ulcers: _____ _____

Colitis: _____ _____

Obesity: _____ _____

Diabetes: _____ _____

Asthma: _____ _____

Cancer: _____ _____

Depression: _____ _____

Anxiety: _____ _____-_____

Bipolar Disorder
(Manic Depression): _____ _____-_____

Alcoholism: _____ _____-_____

Substance Abuse: _____ _____-_____

Obsessive-Compulsive
   Disorder: _____ _____-_____

Anorexia Nervosa: _____ _____-_____

Bulimia: _____ _____-_____

Binge Eating: _____ _____-_____

Gambling: _____ _____-_____

What are the presenting physical symptoms that support a diagnosis of an eating disorder? Please list all those that apply:

(symptoms of anorexia nervosa)

weight loss _____   restrictive eating _____   binge eating _____
vomiting _____   over-exercising _____   bradycardia _____
amenorrhea _____   cold intolerance _____   constipation _____
lanugo _____   hypotension _____   hypothermia _____
muscle atrophy _____   carotenemia _____   arrhythmias _____
delayed gastric emptying _____   nutritional deficiencies _____   elevated LFTs without symptoms _____
mild anemia, not due to iron or folate deficiency _____   electrolyte abnormalities _____
low glucose levels _____   bone density loss _____   osteoporosis _____
low body temperature _____   hair loss _____   muscle cramps/spasms _____

(symptoms of bulimia)

weight fluctuations _____   weight loss _____   weight gain _____
vomiting _____   over-exercise _____   lightheadedness _____
edema _____   chest pain (esophageal reflux) _____
abdominal pain _____   rectal bleeding _____   constipation _____
orthostatic _____   parotid gland enlargement _____
scars on fingers (from vomiting) _____   loss of tooth enamel _____
electrolyte abnormalities _____   menstrual irregularities _____   sore throat _____
muscle cramps/spasms _____

(symptoms of binge eating)

weight gain _____   high blood pressure _____   high blood sugar _____
type II diabetes _____   high cholesterol _____   cardiac stress _____

What are the presenting emotional symptoms that support the diagnosis of an eating disorder? Please check all that apply (as told to you by your patient):

depression _____   anxiety _____   irritability _____
fatigue _____   difficulty sleeping _____   hyperactivity _____
isolating from friends and/or family _____

What are the presenting cognitive symptoms that support the diagnosis of an eating disorder? Please check all that apply (as told to you by your patient):

preoccupation with food _____   preoccupation with weight _____
"feeling fat" _____   having "good" and "bad" foods _____

difficulty and/or refusal to eat:

carbohydrates _____   fats _____
protein _____   dairy _____

having food rituals _____   making excuses why not to eat _____
feeling relieved when you don't eat _____
feeling you have to get food out of your body _____

other (record as told to you): _____

_____

_____

_____

_____

Secondary information important for diagnosis:

1) History of medical hospitalizations and/or surgeries (and dates):

_____

_____

_____

_____

_____

_____

2) History of psychiatric hospitalizations and/or outpatient treatment (and dates):

_____

_____

_____

_____

_____

_____

3) History of physical, emotional, or sexual trauma? _____

4) Current stressors in patients' life? _____

5) Use of alcohol, drugs, cigarettes, and other substances? _____

Physical Exam: (should be filled out for each appointment)

Temperature: _____   Blood pressure: _____ (lying down)

_____ (standing)

Weight: _____ (after voiding)

Height: _____ (taken only at initial visit)

Last menstruation: _____

---

specific tests for anorexia nervosa

Blood glucose level: _____   Blood urea nitrogen (BUN): _____

Complete Blood Count: _____   Creatinine level: _____

Electrolyte Balance: _____   Urinalysis: _____

Thyroid tests (thyroxine, triiodothyronine resin, thyroid-stimulating hormone): _____

Amylase level: _____   Electrocardiogram (ECG): _____

Calcium, magnesium, and phosphorus levels: _____

Liver function tests: _____   Bone Density: _____

Lower extremity edema: _____

specific tests for bulimia

Bilateral parotid gland hypertrophy: _____

Bruises and lacerations of palate and posterior pharynx: _____

Dental issues (eroded enamel, temperature sensitivity, increased cavities, gum disorders): _____

Electrolyte abnormalities: _____   Lower extremity edema: _____

Excessive thirst and increased urination: _____

Orthostatic changes in blood pressure and pulse: _____

Petechial hemorrages of the cornea, soft palate, or face (seen after vomiting): _____

Blood glucose level: _____   Blood urea nitrogen (BUN): _____

Complete Blood Count: _____   Creatinine level: _____

Electrolyte balance: _____   Urinalysis: _____

Electrocardiogram (ECG): _____

Thyroid tests (see tests for anorexia nervosa): _____

tests for binge eating

Blood glucose level: _____   Blood urea nitrogen (BUN): _____

Complete Blood Count: _____   Urinalysis: _____

Thyroid tests (see tests for anorexia nervosa): _____

Overall presentation: _____
_____
_____
_____
_____
_____

Diagnosis: _____
          _____
          _____

Recommendations: _____
_____
_____
_____
_____
_____
_____

Date of next appointment: _____

The Struggle with Change

The goal of this worksheet is to help your patient understand the role the eating disorder is serving for her. In particular, she will explore the cons of change (as well as the pros). Through this exercise, it is hoped that your patient can clearly identify her fears of letting go of the eating disorder, in order to move her onto the next stage of change. Have your patient fill out this worksheet.

Please describe what purpose you believe the eating disorder provides for you. (Example: The eating disorder prevents me from feeling the intense feelings of loneliness I have within).

_____

_____

_____

In the columns below, please list the "pros" and "cons" of your eating disorder.

Pros	Cons
_____	_____
_____	_____
_____	_____
_____	_____
_____	_____
_____	_____
_____	_____
_____	_____
_____	_____

Please check off those behaviors that are warranting change in order for recovery.

preoccupation with food _____   preoccupation with weight _____

"feeling fat" _____   having "good" and "bad" foods _____

difficulty and/or refusal to eat:

carbohydrates _____   fats _____

protein _____   dairy _____

having food rituals _____   making excuses why not to eat _____

feeling relieved when you don't eat _____   feeling you have to get food out of your body _____

other (record as told to you): _____

_____

_____

_____

As a final exercise, please record what negative feelings you may experience if you make changes to the behaviors above.

_____

_____

_____

_____

_____

_____

Getting Ready for Behavioral Change

This worksheet is designed to help patients who are at the stage of Preparation.
The goal is to help the patient define strategies to help facilitate achievement of her medical goals. Once completed, we recommended that the patient bring a copy of this worksheet to her therapist in order for the therapist to help her prepare emotionally, cognitively, and behaviorally for change.

1) What are the medical issues that you feel ready to change? (please circle all those that apply)

    not knowing my weight   knowing my weight

    cutting back on my exercise   increasing my exercise

    returning to exercise   decreasing purging

    decreasing use of laxatives   decreasing weight

    maintaining weight   increasing weight

    other (explain): _____

2) In the spaces below, outline strategies that you can practice for each stated goal.
(Example: *Goal:* Increase exercise
Strategies: Have an extra snack on exercise days, exercise for no more than 30 minutes 2 times per week to start)

Goal: _____

Strategies: _____
_____
_____
_____
_____

Goal: _____

Strategies: _____
_____
_____
_____
_____

Goal: _____

Strategies: _____
_____
_____
_____
_____

Goal: _____

Strategies: _____
_____
_____
_____
_____

Goal: _____

Strategies: _____
_____
_____
_____
_____

Goal: _____

Strategies: _____
_____
_____
_____
_____

Reward Yourself

The goal of this exercise is to help your patient acknowledge her accomplishments without minimizing them when she has had difficulty meeting a goal.

1) Get a glass jar, plastic container, or piggy bank.
2) Decorate the jar or container to your liking (we recommend using permanent markers, colored glue, sparkles, stickers, paint, etc.).
3) Whenever you have fulfilled a daily goal, put a coin (nickel, dime, quarter, or more if you wish) in the jar. DO NOT take coins away for tasks not completed successfully.
4) Do not remove money from this jar for any reason OTHER than to reward yourself. What you may want to do is wait until you have accumulated enough money (and belief in your changes) and do something special for yourself. Reward yourself for work well done!

Relapse Prevention and Intervention Worksheet

The following worksheet is designed to help your patient explore signs of relapse and develop a plan of action to help with relapse prevention.

We recommend that you either complete this worksheet on your own and/or with you treatment team. Once completed, please give a copy of the exercise to all your treatment providers; it will be an important piece of information for all those involved.

Back Step: On the lines below, please identify symptoms or behaviors that you consider to be a *step back* (or a slip) in your recovery. Be specific with regard to frequency and numbers (when significant).

Thought: (Example: Thinking of food in a preoccuping way for 5 consecutive days)

1) _____
2) _____
3) _____
4) _____
5) _____

Feeling: (Example: Not feeling motivated or finding pleasure in activities that would otherwise give pleasure)

1) _____
2) _____
3) _____
4) _____
5) _____

Behavior: (Example: Cutting back on snacks more than once a week)

1) _____
2) _____
3) _____
4) _____
5) _____

Back Fall: On the lines below, please identify symptoms or behaviors that you believe would depict a *back fall* (or relapse in your recovery). As above, please be specific with regard to frequency and numbers, when significant.

Thought: (Example: Thinking of food in a preoccupying way most every day)

1) _____
2) _____
3) _____
4) _____
5) _____

Feeling: (Example: Nothing else matters as long as I am thin)

1) _____
2) _____
3) _____
4) _____
5) _____

Behavior: (Example: No longer following meal plan when it is still needed)

1) _____
2) _____
3) _____
4) _____
5) _____

Fall Down: On the lines below, please identify symptoms or behaviors that you believe would represent *"hitting bottom"* in your recovery. Again, please identify frequency and numbers when significant.

Thought: (Example: Have illogical thinking around food, fat grams, and calories)

1) _____
2) _____
3) _____
4) _____
5) _____

Feeling: (Example: Feeling suicidal)

1) _____
2) _____
3) _____
4) _____
5) _____

Behavior: (Example: Not being able to keep any food inside)

1) _____
2) _____
3) _____
4) _____
5) _____

Psychopharmacological Issues and Management

There are no medications that have been shown in studies to directly treat any eating disorder. It is not clear whether this is because this spectrum of disorders is not physiologically/biochemically induced, or whether it is because at the point of entering treatment the disorder has other psychological layers that don't respond to medication alone. There is, however, an indication and a role for psychopharmacological evaluation and treatment for many patients with an eating disorder.

The usual rule in evaluating psychiatric patients for medication is to first make a diagnosis using the *Diagnostic and Statistical Manual of Mental Disorders* (DSM-IV; American Psychiatric Association, 1994). Once the diagnosis is clear, medications are recommended based on our knowledge about their efficacy in treating the specific disorder. In some cases, diagnosis may not be easily determined, or may be multiple. In these cases, psychiatrists are moving more and more to using medications for symptom management. What this means is that the clinician looks at the patient's symptoms (areas of difficulty) and selects medications that have been known to be helpful with those kinds of symptoms, regardless of the underlying diagnosis.

As has been said, there are no medications for the specific treatment of eating disorders; therefore, when we think about the role of medicine in eating disorders, we move towards symptom management. In addition, there is high comorbidity with all the eating disorders: patients who present with an eating disorder frequently have at least one additional psychiatric disorder (Garfinkel & Walsh, 1997). Medications *are* also used in treating these comorbid disorders, which will be elaborated upon later.

First we will describe the various medications in general, and their role in treating the symptoms of patients with an eating disorder and a comorbid condition. We will not go into detail about the biochemistry or pharmacology of these medications, but will give you the information we feel is most helpful to have in working with your patients.

MEDICATION INDICATIONS

SSRI Antidepressants

The family of Selective Serotonin Reuptake Inhibitors (SSRIs) started with Prozac, marketed in the United States over 10 years ago. Since then many others in the same family have been marketed, and the use for SSRI antidepressants has expanded. While not all of the SSRIs have been formally tested for all diagnoses/disorders, it has been generally shown that if one works for a disorder/symptom, the others will as well.

Prozac was studied for bulimia, and there was some indication that for some patients it led to a marked decrease in the urge to binge and purge. Unfortunately this effect did not seem to persist over time, but can certainly be useful in helping to break a binge/purge cycle and letting the patient feel more in control. In addition, in patients who have recovered, it has been shown that there is a longer time to relapse if the patient is on Prozac (Goldbloom & Olmsted, 1993; Goldstein, Wilson, Ascroft, & al-Banna, 1999).

SSRI medications are also very useful in many kinds of anxiety disorders, and may therefore have a role in decreasing anxiety in the eating disorder patient. They are also the medical treatment of choice for obsessive-compulsive disorder (OCD), and can be helpful in decreasing some of the obsessive preoccupation with food and body image, or with the eating rituals that interfere with normal eating patterns.

Anxiolytics

This is the family of medications that work directly on anxiety symptoms. Most of the medications are in the benzodiazepene (Valium-type) family. The benzodiazepam family, too, can be helpful in treating acute anxiety. One exception, being neither a benzodiazepene or benzodiazepam derivative, is BuSpar, a preventive type of medication.

Since anxiety is a major problem for patients with eating disorders, it is often helpful to get this under control. For patients where the anxiety is fairly constant throughout the day, BuSpar is a good first choice, as it has no addictive potential. In cases where BuSpar doesn't work, or if the benefit is really needed for specific times (such as before or after a meal) or to decrease anxiety that interferes with sleep, the benzodiazepam family might be more useful. Concerns about using this family of medications will be elaborated on later in the Side Effects discussion.

Naltrexone

Naltrexone inhibits the release of chemicals from the opioid centers of the brain, thus blocking the "pleasure" response. In some patients, it has been shown to be helpful in decreasing purging, because it prevents the "high" that patients frequently experience after vomiting.

Antipsychotics

This family of medications was initially used for patients who were psychotic. Psychosis is a complete loss of touch with reality, perhaps involving hallucinations, delusions, or a formal thought disorder. This symptom can come about as part of many kinds of psychiatric illnesses, including schizophrenia, bipolar disorder (manic-depression), posttraumatic stress disorder (PTSD), and others. The antipsychotics work to reduce the psychosis, and also have a large anti-anxiety component. In people with eating disorders, thought processes can often become extremely rigid, not susceptible to challenge or re-channeling. While we do not consider the distorted thoughts to be of a delusional nature, they can frequently border on that. Antipsychotics can be useful in helping patients work on their cognitive distortions and thought patterns, as well as lowering their anxiety level. As with the benzodiazepams, there are some specific concerns about using this kind of medication, which will be addressed in the later sections.

Appetite Enhancers/Inhibitors

These medications have not been shown to be helpful in treating eating disorders. Clinicians who work with patients with eating disorders will not be surprised, as appetite frequently has so little to do with the disorder, especially in the early stages. The lack of control around normal eating is more clearly related to emotional/psychological factors than to hunger itself.

COMORBID CONDITIONS

Many patients with eating disorders also have other diagnosable psychiatric conditions. The most common comorbid conditions include: (a) depression/dysthymia; (b) obsessive-compulsive disorder; (c) social phobia and other anxiety disorders; and (d) substance abuse disorder, particularly in patients with bulimia. In establishing additional diagnoses, it is important to remember that the symptoms have to be separate from symptoms that could be caused by the eating disorder. For example, many patients with eating disorders have preoccupations—which may border on obsessions—with food, weight, body image, exercise, etc. Many also have rituals around eating or exercise. Based on those symptoms, one could not diagnose OCD, because the symptoms are a part of the eating disorder process. In order to meet criteria for a separate OCD diagnosis, there must be other symptoms or behaviors that meet diagnostic criteria.

If, after a careful history, a diagnosis can be made of a comorbid condition, it is appropriate to treat that disorder. While such treatment may not have a direct effect on the eating disorder, it does maximize the patient's ability to cope with the eating disorder, and work on recovery. In some cases it may be difficult to know whether the condition is related to the eating disorder or not. This can be particularly true for depressive disorders. Demoralization, helplessness, and poor self-esteem are frequently an integral part of an eating disorder, but may also become biochemical in nature. In such cases, particularly if the patient is already working in therapy, and if the patient is struggling with recovery, we recommend aggressively trying to treat any other possible disorders. If the medication doesn't work, or causes problems with side effects, it can always be discontinued.

MEDICATION SIDE EFFECTS

If you look through the Physician's Desk Reference, or a pharmacy printout on any medication, you would have to wonder why anyone would risk the multiple potential side effects listed. Fortunately, most people tolerate medications well, with minimal to few side effects. Some factors that might increase the patient's risk of experiencing side effects are: (a) too high a starting dose; (b) too rapid an increase in dosage; (c) concurrent medical conditions; and (d) interactions with other medications. For patients with an eating disorder, low weight and malnutrition also predispose them to being sensitive to medication side effects. As such, it is often best to start lower and increase slower than with non-compromised patients.

The most common adverse effects patients experience with psychotropic medications (i.e., those that work directly on the brain) are (a) dry mouth, (b) gastrointestinal problems (e.g., nausea, stomachache, constipation, or diarrhea), (c) sedation or (d) activation (i.e., increased energy, irritability, trouble with sleep). Also common are complaints of headache, and light-headedness or dizziness. In low-weight patients, the dizziness/light-headedness and sedation seem to occur more frequently than in other patients. As constipation is already a frequent problem, this can get worse. In patients who purge, the GI discomfort of the medication may be exaggerated by the damage already done to the gastrointestinal tract. Many medications cause an increase in appetite. For virtually all patients with eating disorders, this is very anxiety-provoking and can be counterproductive to their treatment.

As many medication side effects are also the same symptoms that can occur anyway in someone with an eating disorder, it is often hard to know which is the culprit for any particular problem. Cutting back slightly on the medication and watching what happens over the next couple of weeks can sometimes clarify whether the medication is actually responsible, and patients are often willing to try this if they are assured that the medication will be adjusted if found "guilty."

Specific adverse effects will not be detailed here, but some particular cautions should be addressed: When using the anxiolytic medications, it is important to remember that they carry a high risk of abuse or addiction. Because of this, they need to be used under very controlled and monitored conditions, and should be avoided in patients with multiple impulse dyscontrol problems or substance use/abuse.

Antipsychotic medications can be very effective, but due to their potency they are also prone to causing adverse effects. In addition to the general ones mentioned above, muscle stiffness or rigidity may occur; these are called Parkinsonian side effects, due to their mimicking symptoms of Parkinson's Disease. These symptoms will go away with a decrease or discontinuation of the medication.

Another condition that has been associated with the use of most antipsychotics is tardive dyskinesia (TD). TD is a disorder where the patient experiences involuntary muscle movements in the extremities, facial muscles, or trunk. Unlike spasms, these movements are smooth and start out rather small. TD seems to be most implicated in patients who are on antipsychotics for a long period of time, or who require very large doses. Once it appears, it never entirely disappears. Because of this, and the difficult side-effect profile, antipsychotics are used with extra caution.

One medication that should be avoided for patients with eating disorders is Wellbutrin. This is a good antidepressant, but has been associated with the development of seizures in patients with eating disorders.

ISSUES IN MEDICATION MANAGEMENT

Once a diagnosis/diagnoses has been made, the physician embarks on a plan of medication trials. What the physician is looking for is whether the medication is helpful with the targeted symptoms, and whether there are any problems that the medication is causing (adverse reactions or side effects). The only way a physician can accurately evaluate the positive and negative effects of a medication is if the patient takes it as directed.

Compliance (adherence to the directions) is affected by many things. It is perfectly normal for even the best-intentioned person to forget to take medication. Usually, a single dose missed within a week's time will not make a clinical difference, but missing more than that can reduce the efficacy of the medicine. For most medications, remembering to take a dose later on in the day is fine, but this needs to be discussed with the physician for each medication.

For most patients, taking psychiatric medication is a frightening idea. They are upset about having a "mental disease," they don't want to be considered "crazy," or they feel that it is a weakness not to be able to overcome their emotional difficulties on their own. For patients with eating disorders, additional issues may play a role in how compliant they are with medication recommendations.

Control is frequently a large psychological issue for patients with eating disorders. The idea of taking a pill that can "control" them is very frightening, even if it might help. Many patients are ambivalent about accepting help; although they are in distress, they are not ready to give up their eating disorder symptoms. Concerns about side effects play a role for all patients, but eating disorder patients are particularly frightened of possible appetite effects of the medication. In addition, the idea of swallowing a pill can be difficult for someone who is having difficulty eating normally and nourishing herself.

Other issues may affect patients with eating disorders. Patients who purge may not be getting the full effects of their medication; if a patient vomits before the medicine has had a chance to get fully absorbed into the system, it reduces the efficacy of that specific pill. Another problem relates to taking medications with meals. Fortunately, few of these medications need to be taken with food, but some medications are better tolerated if they are taken with meals. If a patient is restricting, this may not be an option, and the patient may not be able to stick with the medication due to discomfort.

MEDICATION EFFICACY

The efficacy of medication depends on the specific medication, and the disorder for which it is being used. Studies that look at this usually focus on clearly agreed-upon diagnoses with few complicating factors. The best studies then compare two groups of people—those who receive the trial medication, and those who receive a placebo (a pill that pretends to be medication, but really has no active medication in it).

In clinical practice, we are often presented with patients whose symptoms are not always so clear, and we rarely have the ability to conduct a placebo-controlled trial for any patient. What we are left with is our best judgment about which medications might help with which symptoms, and then we embark on a clinical trial for that particular patient. So while we know that antidepressants can be very helpful in at least 70% of patients with major depression, that says nothing specific about whether our patient will benefit from the medication, or even be able to tolerate it.

Many practitioners also find that patients with eating disorders, especially low-weight patients, are less responsive to medication than would be expected. Perhaps this is because the degree of malnourishment prevents the brain or body from reacting to the medication. Perhaps the symptoms we are trying to treat are really due to physical malnutrition rather than a psychiatric disorder. Or perhaps there is something about a person with an eating disorder that predisposes her to be less responsive to the effects of medication. At this time we don't really know the answer to this dilemma, but it certainly must always be in the practitioner's mind.

If a patient is not responding to a medication, one must first look at the compliance with taking the medication. If the patient is responsibly following the plan, the next thing to think about is whether the dose of the medication is appropriate. In some cases, medication blood levels may be helpful in tracking whether the body is metabolizing the medication appropriately, and whether the dose is in the therapeutic range. In other cases, we push the dose up to the highest one possible, without causing uncomfortable side effects.

The other aspect of monitoring efficacy is the length of time to look for a response. Patients will frequently want to give up on a medication if they don't feel better right away; educating them as to the need for dosage adjustment and appropriate length of treatment is very important. Medications may have some effect within a couple of weeks, but frequently need from 4 to 12 weeks for the practitioner to know whether they are going to work. One also needs to look for *partial response;* patients may have some small improvements, even though there are no dramatic changes.

If you feel satisfied that a patient has given a medication a fair trial (i.e., taken it regularly at the right dose for the necessary amount of time) and is having no response, the responsible thing is to stop the medication, usually by tapering it down. It does not help to have patients on any medications from which they don't benefit, and doing so can make further medication management more complicated. In addition, if a patient knows that you are going to be thoughtful, active, and practical in evaluating medication efficacy, she or he is more likely to be a willing partner with you in your search for a helpful medication.

THE ROLE OF THE NON-MEDICAL CLINICIAN
IN MEDICATION MANAGEMENT

The clinician who works with an eating disorder patient frequently finds her/himself in the position of being a case manager. In addition to working therapeutically with the patient, the clinician is frequently the one to monitor and coordinate other aspects of care.

The first job of the clinician is frequently to recognize the need for a psychiatric/medication evaluation. Many patients will see a non-medical clinician first, may have resisted prior recommendations for medication, or may be receiving inadequate medication treatment or follow-up. I generally recommend that all eating disorders patients receive a thorough psychopharmacological evaluation. Even if medication is not indicated, or if the patient is adamant about refusing medication, some psychoeducation around medication issues can still go a long way. I always review with patients the indications for medication, the rationale, the possibilities, and whether or not I recommend them for that specific person. I like patients to know from the start what the options are, because then they can keep them in mind as part of their overall treatment plan. In addition, if you don't push the medication initially, but just use the time to educate the patient, then she can make an informed decision about her treatment, rather than reacting out of fear, misinformation, or oppositionality.

Once a patient is on medication, the primary clinician or individual therapist is in a good position to monitor compliance. Seeing the patient on a regular basis provides a good, frequent check-in as to whether the patient is taking the medication and keeping medical appointments. The prescribing physician may not see the patient more than once every month or two, and, thus the PCC or therapist is in a better position to watch and listen for information from the patient that indicates the medication is or is not working.

Patients are also more likely to confide in non-medical clinicians any problems they are having with taking their medications, including fears and side effects. This clinician can then encourage the patient to call the prescribing physician, bring it up at the next meeting, or the clinician can convey the information directly to the prescriber. The primary clinician or therapist can also offer a more objective view as to medication efficacy. Patients may under- or overevaluate the effect of medication, while clinicians can monitor behavioral and emotional changes.

A final, very important role that the PCC has, with respect to medications, is to monitor the patient's risk level. If a patient is suicidal, or misusing/abusing medications, the prescriber needs to know that, and a safety plan needs to be put into place. The clinician can help the patient figure out a plan that allows for her or him to continue to take the medication, but in a more supervised or controlled way, until the risk diminishes.

For clients with eating disorders, medication is not a panacea. Research evidence indicates that medication in combination with cognitive behavioral therapy is more effective than medication alone for most clients (Jimerson, Herzog, & Brotman, 1993), especially in the beginning phases of treatment. Primary clinicians or therapists are the arbiters, most frequently, of their client's choice of treatment options. A psychopharmacological evaluation from a psychiatrist, if not recommended by the primary clinician or therapist, may not be recommended by anyone else. Recommending a psychopharmacological evaluation, whether or not you believe medication should be prescribed, is clinically responsible and prudent in the treatment of most clients with eating disorders. Even if medication is not indicated during the initial consultation, learning about medication's potential benefits in the treatment of the frequently seen comorbid conditions associated with eating disorders, or for help in reducing eating disorders' symptoms, can be helpful to your client in the future.

If a psychiatrist with eating disorders expertise is not available in your area, consultation with the patient's primary care doctor (PCP) or nurse clinician, is recommended. Many clients receive appropriate medication information and assessment from their PCPs. When consultation or referral to a psychiatrist, especially one with eating disorders expertise, is possible, however, we recommend that a referral to such a provider be included in the assessment and treatment plan of most eating disorders clients.

THE STAGES OF CHANGE AND MEDICATION

Here is a quick guide concerning clients' stages of change and issues of medication.

Precontemplation Stage

For the client in Precontemplation, we recommend that the primary care clinician and the primary therapist educate the client about the potential benefits of medication for the eating disorder symptoms and other comorbid diagnoses of the client. Clients at this stage of change are generally not motivated to accept the diagnosis/diagnoses or they are in the clinician's office under duress. A warm, receptive, non-judgmental approach by the clinician along with education is what clients at the stage of Precontemplation need and can use.

Contemplation Stage

For the client in the stage of Contemplation, exploring the pros and cons of a psychopharmacological assessment is the goal. Many clients at this stage know that they have an eating disorder. Some may understand that they may suffer from other comorbid conditions as well. At this stage, many clients need to talk about their ambivalence concerning taking medications. Many fear that medications could control them or could intensify their appetite or cause unchecked weight gain. Some fear that medication will make any progress "not mine." They believe that their personality will change. They fear some outside force will propel them into a change process before they are ready. Some fear putting anything into their mouths.

Clients at this stage must explore all their fears and ambivalent feelings in an open and accepting environment. Once this is done, they will need reassurance from you that even if they choose to go for an initial psychopharmacological evaluation appointment with a psychiatrist, they will not be compelled to take medication even if it is recommended. Only when clients can trust that they will have a choice about whether or not to take medication will they seek psychopharmacological consultation.

Once the consultation takes place, you and your client can talk about the pros and cons of taking versus not taking the recommended medication.

Preparation Stage

The client in Preparation has decided with you that taking the medication is the right choice for her. She must then prepare a plan which supports her efforts to try the medication. These plans might include keeping a schedule indicating when and how much medication to take. The two of you can develop a chart to check off each time she takes the medication. If she is at risk for purging the medication, you and she can talk with the prescribing physician to determine if the medication can be taken at a time when the client is less likely to purge. You can also use her desire to try medication as an impetus to work on reducing purging urges and delaying purges even when the urges are strong. Once the plan is in place the client is ready for Action, the actual taking of the medication.

Action Stage

The client in the stage of Action is taking the medication. At this stage the client will need to talk with you about her thoughts, feelings, and fears about embarking on this road. She will need to regularly review with you whether or not she is taking the medication as prescribed and whether she is holding the medication down. These clients also need to look at whether or not they are caring for themselves in ways which will maximize the chances that the medication will be effective. These include monitoring whether the client is using other drugs or alcohol and whether the client is eating, sleeping, and attending her regular appointments with her primary care physician and nurse for medical monitoring. Finally, you and the client must monitor the potential benefits and side effects of the medication. This step is critically important as you may see the client more frequently than the prescribing physician. You and your client will need to decide who will tell the prescriber of benefits or problems related to the medication. Any troublesome side effects, problems with compliance, or changes in mental status or physical health must be reported to the prescribing physician immediately to protect the well-being of your client.

Maintenance Stage

The client in Maintenance will be taking her medication regularly and as prescribed. She will have found the medication and dosage that is right for her. When you see the client you and she should regularly discuss how she is doing on the medication so, once again, any problems can be reported to the prescribing physician.

Once your client is ready for Termination, if she continues on medication, she will directly discuss her medication issues with her psychiatrist.

CONCLUSION

Over the years we have heard professionals express frustration when treating clients with eating disorders. Many felt their efforts were for naught, no matter what theoretical stance they took or how many hours they spent with a client. They did not see movement toward recovery in the number they had hoped. Prochaska et al.'s (1994) Stages of Change theory offers mental health professionals, physicians, nurses, registerd dieticians, and all others who work with clients with eating disorders a new template and hope. Stages of Change theory tells us that people, all people, change problem behaviors in a consistent manner. They follow the stages sequentially, and our task as clinicians is to match our intervention to each client's stage of change. Furthermore, it tells us that each stage is equal in value to the next. Thus, the act of changing, like the act of growing—often imperceptible to the observer—is occurring if we nurture each client with the appropriate intervention at each stage. The client who does not see herself as eating disordered can still benefit from our educational intervention as long as it is done in a relational, non-judgmental fashion. The client who knows her eating disorder is a problem but cannot fathom living life without it, will be surprised and calmed when we tell her that we realize that her eating disorder has helped her, even though it is now hurting her. The client who is ready to act will feel reassured when we say we will help her prepare her battle plans rather than rushing her into action. The client in action will reduce her harsh self-statements when we define her progress as well as set-backs as opportunities to learn. Clients are amazed to hear that we do not expect them to do everything perfectly or immediately.

Stages of Change theory helps clients and therapists understand what is needed at the time and encourages faith in the self and the change process. Many clients are reassured to learn that they do not have to have an equal stage of readiness for each problematic behavior. While working on one behavior, they might find themselves incredulous that another, not targeted for change, is changing anyway. Appreciating readiness for change, attending to the tasks at each stage, and trusting that clients will progress if given the time and support to grow in readiness encourages hope.

In fact it is hope, the hope that a client once desperately ill will walk into your office as one walked into ours, displaying radiant health and happiness and stating, "I became well because you helped me do what I was ready and able to do. You respected and supported me when I made progress and when I slipped back. You had faith in me when I had no faith in myself. You told me I could recover and I did when it was *my* time to change."

References

American Psychiatric Association. (1994). *Diagnostic and statistical manual of mental disorders* (4th ed.). New York: Author.

Bulik, C. M., Sullivan, P. F., Epstein, L. H., McKee, M., Kaye, W. H., Dahl, R. E., & Weltzin, T. E. (1992). Drug use in women with anorexia and bulimia nervosa. *International Journal of Eating Disorders, 11*(3), 213–225.

Evans, K., & Sullivan, J. M. (1995). *Treating addicted survivors of trauma.* New York: Guilford.

Garfinkel, P. E., & Walsh, B. T. (1997). *Drug therapies.* In: *Handbook of treatment of eating disorders,* 2nd ed., (pp. 372–380). New York: Guilford.

Goldbloom, D. S., & Olmsted, M. P. (1993). Pharmacotherapy of bulimia nervosa with fluoxetine: Assessment of clinically significant attitudinal change. *American Journal of Psychiatry, 150,* 770–774.

Goldstein, D. J., Wilson, M. G., Ascroft, R. C., & al-Banna, M. (1999). Effectiveness of fluoxetine therapy in bulimia nervosa regardless of comorbid depression. *International Journal of Eating Disorders, 25*(1), 19–27.

Goodman, L., & Villapiano, M. (2001). *Eating disorders: The journey to recovery workbook.* Philadelphia: Brunner-Routledge.

Helm, K. K., & Klawitter, B. (1995). *Nutrition therapy: Advanced counseling skills.* Lake Dallas, TX: Helm Seminars.

Herman, J. L. (1992). *Trauma and recovery.* New York: Basic Books.

Hirschmann, J. R., & Munter, C. H. (1988). *Overcoming overeating: Living free in a world of food.* New York: Fawcett Columbine.

Jimerson, D. C., Herzog, D. B., & Brotman, A. W. (1993). Pharmacologic appraches in the treatment of eating disorders. *Harvard Review of Psychiatry, 1,* 82–93.

Keys, A., Brozek, J., Henschel, A., Mickelsen, O., & Taylor, H. L. (1950). *The biology of human starvation* (2 vols.). Minneapolis: University of Minnesota Press.

Linehan, M. M. (1993a). *Skills training manual for treating borderline personality disorder.* New York: Guilford.

Linehan, M. M. (1993b). *Cognitive-behavioral treatment of borderline personality disorder.* New York: Guilford.

Miller, K. J. (1996). Prevalence and process of disclosure of childhood sexual abuse among eating-disordered women. In M. F. Schwartz & L. Cohn (Eds.), *Sexual abuse and eating disorders* (pp. 36–51). Philadelphia: Brunner/Mazel.

Pribor, E. F., & Dinwiddie, S. H. (1992). Psychiatric correlates of incest in childhood. *American Journal of Psychiatry, 149,* 52–56.

Prochaska, J. O., Norcross, J. C., & DiClemente, C. C. (1994). *Changing for good.* New York: William Morrow.

Shaw, A., Fulton, L., Davis, C., & Hogbin, M. (1996). *Using the food pyramid: A resource for nutrition educators.* U.S. Department of Agriculture, Food, Nutrition, and Consumer Services, and Center for Nutrition Policy and Promotion.

V., Rachel (1987). A conversation with Marion Woodman on addiction and spirituality. In *Rachel V., Family secrets: Life stories of adult children of alcoholics* (pp. 144–150). San Francisco: Harper & Row.

Villapiano, A. (1999). *Workshop handouts. Innovative Training Systems.* Newton, MA.

Recommended Reading

Agras, W. S., & Apple, R. F. (1997). *Overcoming eating disorders: Therapist guide.* San Antonio: The Psychological Corporation.

Bass, E., & Davis, L. (1988). *The courage to heal: A guide for women survivors of child sexual abuse.* New York: Harper & Row.

Brewerton, T. D., Lydiard, R. B., Herzog, D. B., Brotman, A. W., O'Neil, P. M., & Ballenger, J. D. (1995). Comorbidity of axis I psychiatric disorders in bulimia nervosa. *Journal of Clinical Psychiatry, 56*(2), 77–80.

Bulik, C. M. (1987). Alcohol use and depression in women with bulimia. *American Journal of Drug and Alcohol Abuse, 13*(3), 343–355.

Bulik, C. M, Sullivan, P. F., Fear, J. L., & Joyce, P. R. (1997). Eating disorders and antecedent anxiety disorders: A controlled study. *Acta Psychiatry Scandinavia, 96*(2), 101–107.

deZwaan, M., & Mitchell, J. E. (1992). Opiate antagonists and eating behavior in humans: A review. *Journal of Clinical Pharmacology, 32,* 1060–1072.

Fairburn, D. (1995). *Overcoming binge eating.* New York: Guilford.

Fluoxetine Bulimia Nervosa Collaborative Study Group. (1992). Fluozetine in the treatment of bulimia nervosa. *Archives of General Psychiatry, 49,* 139–147.

Franko, D. L. (1997). Ready or not? Stages of change as predictors of brief group therapy outcome in bulimia nervosa. *Group, 21*(1), 39–45.

Garfinkel, P. E., & Garner, D. M. (Eds.). (1987). *The role of drug treatments for eating disorders.* New York: Brunner/Mazel.

Garner, D. M., & Garfinkel, P. E. (Eds.). (1997). *Handbook of treatment for eating disorders* (2nd ed.). New York: Guilford.

Gwirtsman, H. E., Guze, B. H., Yager, J., & Gainsley, B. (1990). Fluozetine treatment of anorexia nervosa: An open clinical trial. *Journal of Clinical Psychiatry, 51,* 378–382.

Hall, L., & Ostroff, M. (1999). *Anorexia nervosa: A guide to recovery.* Carlsbad, CA: Gurze Books.

Hall, L. (1992). *Bulimia nervosa: A guide to recovery.* Carlsbad, CA: Gurze Books.

Jonas, J. M., & Gold, M. S. (1988). The use of opiate antagonists in treating bulimia: A study of low-dose versus high-dose naltrexone. *Psychiatry Resident, 24*(2), 195–199.

Jonas, J. M., Gold, M. S., Sweney, D., & Pottash, A. L. C. (1987). Eating disorders and cocaine abuse: A survey of 259 cocaine abusers. *Journal of Clinical Psychiatry, 48*(2), 47–50.

Kaplan, A. S., & Garfinkel, P. E. (1993). *Medical issues and the eating disorders: The interface.* New York: Brunner/Mazel.

Kirby, J. (1998). *Dieting for dummies.* Foster City, CA: IDG Books.

Marrazzi, M. A., Kinzie, J., & Luby, E. D. (1995). A detailed longitudinal analysis on the use of naltrexone in the treatment of bulimia. *International Clinical Psychopharmacology, 10*(3), 173–176.

Mitchell, J. E., Pyle, R., Eckert, E. D., & Hatsukami, D. (1990). The influence of prior alcohol and drug abuse problems on bulimia nervosa treatment outcome. *Addictive Behavior, 15,* 169–173.

Mitchell, J. E., Pyle, R. L., Eckert, E. D., Hatsukami, D., Pomeroy, C., & Zimmerman, R. (1990). A comparison study of antidepressants and structured intensive group psychotherapy in the treatment of bulimia nervosa. *Archives of General Psychiatry, 47,* 149–157.

Schmidt, U., & Treasure, J. (1997). *Getting better bit(e) by bit(e): Clinician's guide.* London: Psychology Press.

Schuckit, M. A., Tipp, J. E., Anthenelli, R. M., Bucholz, K. K., Hesselbrock, V. M., & Nurnberger, J. I., Jr. (1996). Anorexia nervosa and bulimia nervosa in alcohol-dependent men and women and their relatives. *American Journal of Psychiatry, 153,* 74–82.

Schwartz, M. F., & Cohn, L. (Eds.). (1996). *Sexual abuse and eating disorders.* New York: Brunner/Mazel.

Selby, M. J., & Moreno, K. (1995). Personal and familial substance misuse patterns among eating disordered and depressed subjects. *International Journal of the Addictions, 30*(9), 1169–1176.

Siegel, M., Brisman, J., & Weinshel, M. (1988). *Surviving an eating disorder: Strategies for family and friends.* New York: Harper & Row.

Striegel-Moore, R. H., Garvin, V., Dohm, F. A., & Rosenheck, R. A. (1999). Eating disorders in a national sample of hospitalized female and male veterans: Detection rates and psychiatric comorbidity. *International Journal of Eating Disorders, 25*(4), 405–414.

Thiel, A., Broocks, A., Ohlmeier, M., Jacoby, G. E., & Schufsler, G. (1995). Obsessive-compulsive disorder among patients with anorexia nervosa and bulimia nervosa. *American Journal of Psychiatry, 152,* 72–75.

Thornton, C., & Russell, J. (1997). Obsessive compulsive comorbidity in the dieting disorders. *International Journal of Eating Disorders, 21*(1), 83–87.

Walsh, B. T., Hadigan, C. M., Devlin, M. J., Gladis, M., & Roose, S. P. (1991). Long-term outcome of antidepressant treatment for bulimia nervosa. *American Journal of Psychiatry, 148,* 1206–1212.

Watts, W. D., & Ellis, A. M. (1992). Drug abuse and eating disorders: preventive implications. *Journal of Drug Education, 22*(3), 223–240.

Yates, A. (1991). *Compulsive exercise and the eating disorders.* New York: Brunner/Mazel.

Zerbe, K. J. (1995). *The body betrayed: A deeper understanding of women, eating disorders, and treatment.* Carlsbad, CA: Gurze Books.

Index

A

abuse 12
    sexual 51, 99–110
action stage 2–3, 45, 54, 65, 77, 83, 105–106, 117, 141, 165–166
addiction 92–98
affirmations 103
al-Banna, M. 160
alcohol 92–96
amenorrhea 51, 75, 136, 143
antipsychotics 160
anorexia 42, 81, 82, 113–114, 136–137
anxiolytics 160
appetite enhancers 161
artistic expression 103
Ascroft, R. C. 160
athlete 81–89
attire, therapist's 8

B

behavioral change 154
beverages, therapist's 9–10
binge eating 61–72, 130
biological issues 52
bipolar disorder 160
body image 73–80
body messages 8
bone density 143
Brozek, J. 53
Bulik, C. M. 93, 95
bulimia 42, 61–72, 81–82, 92, 93, 96–98, 136, 160, 161
BuSpar 160

C

case load 14
child development 41, 50–51, 81
client, matching with treatment 1–2
cocaine 91
collaboration 13
comorbid conditions 161
consultation 14, 22
contemplation stage 2–3, 44, 53, 62, 66, 75–76, 83, 95, 96, 100–102, 140, 165
continuing care 143
contract
    patient 144
    therapeutic 13–14
cultural issues 10, 50

D

Dahl, R. E. 93, 95
Davis, C. 111
decisional balance 95
demand feeding 41
depression 161
deprivation 43
diagnosis, initial 136–138
Diagnostic and Statistical Manual of Mental Disorders 159
DiClemente, C. C. xiii, 1–4, 95, 166
Dinwiddie, S. H. 99
dysthymia 161

E

eating, healthy 42–43
Epstein, L. H. 93, 95
Evans, K. 92–93

F

family issues 50–51
follow-up visits 142–143
food 49–60
    fear of 49–54
    punishment 41–42
    pyramid 111–112
    restriction 49–54
    reward 41–42
    therapists and 9–10
Fulton, L. 111
funnel questioning 99

G

gender, therapist's 11
Goldbloom, *not in references* 160
Goldstein, D. J. 160

H

H.A.L.T. 45
Helm, Kathy King 113
Henschel, A. 53
Herman, Judith 100
Hirschmann, Jane 42, 43
Hogbin, M. 111
Hospitalization 142–143
hunger 41–48
    cultural 43
    social 42